Wronged by Empire

Studies in Asian Security

The **Studies in Asian Security** book series promotes analysis, understanding, and explanation of the dynamics of domestic, transnational, and international security challenges in Asia. The peer-reviewed publications in the Series analyze contemporary security issues and problems to clarify debates in the scholarly community, provide new insights and perspectives, and identify new research and policy directions. Security is defined broadly to include the traditional political and military dimensions as well as nontraditional dimensions that affect the survival and well being of political communities. Asia, too, is defined broadly to include Northeast, Southeast, South, and Central Asia.

Designed to encourage original and rigorous scholarship, books in the Studies in Asian Security series seek to engage scholars, educators, and practitioners. Wide-ranging in scope and method, the Series is receptive to all paradigms, programs, and traditions, and to an extensive array of methodologies now employed in the social sciences.

Wronged by Empire

POST-IMPERIAL IDEOLOGY AND
FOREIGN POLICY IN INDIA AND CHINA

Manjari Chatterjee Miller

STANFORD UNIVERSITY PRESS
Stanford, California

Stanford University Press
Stanford, California

© 2013 by the Board of Trustees of the
Leland Stanford Junior University
All rights reserved

Printed in the United States of America

Library of Congress Cataloging-in-Publication Data

Miller, Manjari Chatterjee, author.
    Wronged by empire : post-imperial ideology and foreign policy in India and
China / Manjari Chatterjee Miller.
        pages cm. — (Studies in Asian security)
    Includes bibliographical references and index.
    ISBN 978-0-8047-8652-2 (cloth : alk. paper)
    ISBN 978-0-8047-9338-4 (pbk. : alk. paper)
        1. India—Foreign relations—1984–. 2. India—Foreign relations—1947–1984.
3. China—Foreign relations—1949–. 4. Imperialism—Psychological aspects. 5.
Imperialism—Psychological aspects.. I. Title. III. Series: Studies in Asian security.
    DS448.M46 2013
    327.51—dc23   2013010530

    ISBN 978-0-8047-8843-4 (electronic)

This book is printed on acid-free, archival-quality paper.

Typeset at Stanford University Press in 10/13.5 Bembo

For BABA *and* MA

Contents

Figures, Maps and Tables

Figures

Maps

Tables

Acknowledgments

There are two people without whom this book would never have been written. Roderick McFarquhar, a walking encyclopedia on *both* India and China, persuaded me to study Mandarin ("It's really not very hard"), compete for language fellowships ("There's always money, you just have to look"), and go talk to Alastair Iain Johnston ("He's brilliant"). It turns out he was 70 percent right and 30 percent wrong (learning Mandarin *was* very hard). I will forever be grateful to Iain Johnston who was an incredible advisor and a source of professional and personal support. Rod and Iain encouraged me to study India and China at a time when comparisons of the two were not fashionable, and Iain nurtured and sustained my interest. Thank you.

This book has been completed at four universities and in three countries. I received support and advice from three amazing people I met at Harvard—Stephen Peter Rosen, Sugata Bose and Allan Stam who were always there for me. Andrew Kennedy, Michael Horowitz, Asif Efrat, Stephen Levitsky, Jorge Dominguez, Pär Cassel, Warigia Bowman, Fotini Christia, Daniel Sargent, Zhenzhen Lu, Gokul Madhavan and Gordon Harvey provided valuable feedback. Luci Herman, Lauren Brandt, Elizabeth Mellyn, Alexander Noonan and Brett Flehinger wrote with me, read and re-read drafts, and made me explain my arguments to an interdisciplinary audience. The Weatherhead Center, Fairbank Center and South Asia Initiative funded language and research trips and provided a forum for receiving feedback. Thank you.

At Princeton, Tom Christensen, Yinan He, Lynn T. White, Gil Rozman, Todd Hall and David Leheny gave excellent comments. The China and the World

Program at the Woodrow Wilson School provided logistical and financial support. At the University of Pennsylvania's Center for the Advanced Study of India, the comments of Devesh Kapur and Avery Goldstein helped polish the final draft. And at Boston University, I had the support of my department and excellent students, particularly Todd Fowler, Claudia Huang and Ling Jie. Thank you.

In India and China, I benefited from the time and patience of S. K. Singh, J. N. Dixit, C. V. Ranganathan, I. K. Gujral, P. V. Narasimha Rao, Jagat Mehta, C. Raja Mohan, Natwar Singh, Niu Jun, Cai Jiahe, Zhang Baijia, Wang Yizhou and Zhao Yuguang. The staff at the Nehru Memorial Archives in Delhi were efficient and a pleasure to work with. I owe a special debt to my Chinese teachers at Middlebury, Princeton-in-Beijing, IUP-Berkeley and Harvard, especially Wang *laoshi*, Peng *laoshi* and *da* Zhang *laoshi*. Thank you.

The editors at Stanford University Press: Studies in Asian Security—Muthiah Alagappa, Amitav Acharya, David Leheny and Geoffrey Burn—were wonderful. The East-West Center provided financial support. And Christopher Clary patiently read and commented on the manuscript in detail. Thank you.

I relied on an extremely supportive family. My parents have always believed in me more than I have believed in myself and never questioned my education or career choices. I was fortunate that I gained in-laws who understood the academic path and *never* asked when this book would be done. And both my parents and in-laws logged in countless hours of patient babysitting while I researched and wrote. Thank you.

I was lucky enough to marry my best friend and counsel, and even luckier, that we now enjoy two beautiful children who help prioritize my day. This book would not have been started, continued or finished without Jeff's support. *Thank you.*

Wronged by Empire

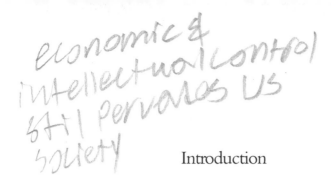
economic &
intellectual control
still pervades US
society

Introduction

We are often told "Colonialism is dead." Let us not be deceived or even soothed by that. I say to you, colonialism is not yet dead. How can we say it is dead, so long as vast areas of Asia and Africa are unfree?

And, I beg of you do not think of colonialism only in the classic form which we of Indonesia, and our brothers in different parts of Asia and Africa, knew. Colonialism has also its modern dress, in the form of economic control, intellectual control, actual physical control by a small but alien community within a nation. It is a skillful and determined enemy, and it appears in many guises. It does not give up its loot easily. Wherever, whenever and however it appears colonialism is an evil thing, and one which must be eradicated from the earth. . . .

President Sukarno, Speech at the Opening of the Bandung Conference, April 18, 1955

The phenomenon of colonial empires encompassing far-flung territorial possessions ended more than half a century ago with the decolonization of large numbers of states, and the carving out of entirely new countries. But the legacy of colonialism endures in cultural, economic, and political ways. Extractive colonialism cut a deep and bloody path through the history of the erstwhile colonies, leaving behind disputed borders, territorial conflicts, and lasting economic inequities.[1]

If the practice of colonialism altered the political, economic, cultural and historical trajectory of the colonized countries, then its dissolution arguably created an ideational shift in the international system.[2] Owning colonies had been an unquestionable "right" that over a few decades became an indisputable "wrong."[3] The end of colonialism was not just a mere redistribution of power in the international system. Colonizers became unable to hold on to their colonies because the *very idea of colonies became morally unacceptable.*[4] As a result, countries that had experienced colonialism burst on the international scene in a new avatar, with leaders who had strong anti-colonial nationalist credentials, contested and often blood-soaked, political boundaries, a desire to create a new international order, and a very strong sense of personal and collective *suffering* under colonial domination.

The transformative historical event of colonialism was, to these nations, a very negative one. By this I mean it was treated and responded to as collective trauma. These states, despite the wide variation in colonial experience, believed themselves to be *victims* of colonial domination. The political narrative they wove emphasized the wrongs they had suffered and the quest for restitution.

Consequently, two new arguments form the basis of this book. First, I argue that the study of international relations is radically incomplete if it fails to account systematically for colonialism and its legacy. Drawing on literature from the field of psychology, I show that colonialism was a transformative historical event that ex-colonies regarded and responded to as collective historical trauma.

Second, I show that this large category of actors—states that have undergone the traumatic transformative historical event of extractive colonialism—maintain an emphasis on victimhood and entitlement that dominates their decision calculus even today. I argue that they have a "post-imperial ideology," or PII, that drives their international behavior. PII comprises a sense of victimization that brings with it a dominant goal to be recognized and empathized with as a victim by others in the international system. I refer to this as the goal of victimhood, which is simultaneously a desire to be recognized as a victim and also to ensure that one will not be victimized again in the future. This dominant goal drives two subordinate goals: maximizing territorial sovereignty and maximizing status. These three goals are inherent in PII, and their pursuit shapes foreign policy in states that hold such beliefs. This analysis is a dramatic departure from conventional international relations explanations of state behavior. Specifically, I focus on India and China, states that are usually analyzed as rising powers, and show that despite very different colonial experiences, they share a similar emphasis on victimhood that drives their foreign policy decisions.

Dominant theories of state behavior in the international system, such as realism and neo-realism, are drawn largely from nineteenth-century world power politics in Europe and America and focus on power and security as the main motivators of behavior. The emphasis is on security calculations in response to military threats. Liberal theories usually focus on the domestic competition between, and influence of, different actors within society. The theoretical assumption is that the logic of political survival dictates domestic politics and, therefore, political survival is the primary incentive driving governments. World systems theories, many with explicitly Marxist influences, have focused broadly on extractive imperialism and colonialism, but have done so in terms of its systemic effects, particularly economic dependency and exploitation, and as a consequence have focused on the motivations of the colonizing states.[5]

These theoretical stances do not and can not systematically treat colonialism as a variable influencing the behavior of states. Neither do they give weight to ideology or beliefs drawn from transformative historical events that could influence state behavior. This, despite ample work in the psychology literature detailing the importance of individual memory, collective memory and inter-generational transmission, and the connection between the individual, the collective and the development of societal institutions.

Moreover, theories of offensive and defensive realism with predictions of state behavior such as balancing, bandwagoning, or bargaining refer primarily to states with material capabilities significant enough to matter, while norm-based theories focus on states with the ability to impose or break norms—obviously, norms held by states that are perceived as "successful" (usually Western states) are more likely to be adopted.[6] The behavior of non-Western nations tends to be given short shrift in traditional studies of international relations, and when they do receive attention, the assumption is that disparities in economic structures and material capabilities are the sole basis of distinguishing them from the more developed nations.[7]

This oversight becomes particularly acute when looking at non-Western states, such as India and China, that seek to alter the international status quo. These two countries, home to 37 percent of the world's population, have enormous and growing economic power, military capability, and international clout. Analysts agree that their foreign policy choices are a critical determinant of regional and global security in the twenty-first century. But comparisons of India and China, or analyses of their behavior, often rest on their material capabilities and economic prowess. There is little, if any, credence given to the fact that modern India and China rose from the ashes of their colonial experience and that both countries place enormous importance on their colonial past.

Comparisons of India and China, other than categorizing them as rising powers, often emphasize their numerous economic, political and social differences—their economic trajectory is different; India's growth is service-led, while China's growth is manufacturing-driven;[8] India has had a relatively stable democratic regime for more than fifty years, China is a socialist dictatorship; the bulk of India's population is uncaring of foreign policy,[9] and audience costs related to international behavior are often media and elite-driven,[10] while Chinese domestic audiences often care very much about China's international image and bilateral relationships.[11]

Their experiences of colonialism were also very different, with two hundred years of British rule in India, and piecemeal colonial rule by Western powers and Japan in China. Yet surprisingly, as this book details, the different experiences of colonialism gave rise to independence and post-independence movements that similarly emphasized suffering and loss rather than their eventual victory over colonialism.[12] Thus, despite their many differences, including different colonial experiences, the two nations responded to their colonial history in a similar fashion—as collective trauma. They strongly believed that they had been victimized, and this belief and corresponding sense of entitlement continues to influence their behavior today. Therefore, in order to understand their behavior in international relations today, it is absolutely crucial to understand their colonial past.

This book begins by examining the phenomenon of colonialism and its legacy. Chapter 1 uses trauma theory drawn from the psychology literature to show that the transformative historical event of colonialism in India and China can be classified as collective trauma. In it, I lay out the theoretical foundations of PII and show how it is an essential component of both India's and China's national identity and international outlook. Chapter 2 uses statistical analysis to establish the existence of a discourse of victimhood in countries that have experienced colonialism. It uses a new method to analyze speeches from 1993 to 2007 in the United Nations to show with statistical significance that there is a difference in the discourse of states that have been colonized and those that have not, and that difference is due to a strong sense of victimhood.

Chapters 3, 4, and 5 then turn to specific foreign policy decisions of India and China, discuss the weaknesses of alternative explanations, and use PII as an independent variable to explain policy choices. Chapter 3 makes use of previously unused archival documents to look at the 1960 border negotiations between India and China, the last of such negotiations between the two countries before they went to war in 1962. The chapter outlines how the interaction of the three goals of PII led to the failure of the negotiations and, consequently, a border war that still affects relations between the two countries five decades later. It also shows that PII had already emerged as a recognizable and coherent belief system in these two countries in the years just after decolonization.

Chapter 4 turns to the contemporary period to show that PII and, specifically, victimhood matter today. It analyzes India's decision to declare nuclear weapons state status in 1998. It uses PII to explain why India decided to conduct further nuclear tests after the first halting tests in 1974, and why it conducted them in 1998. To do so, it utilizes thousands of articles in the Indian print media in 1974 and in the 1990s to demonstrate that a sense of victimization and entitlement regarding the nuclear issue did not exist in 1974, but had appeared by the 1998 decision.

Chapter 5 continues in the contemporary period and focuses on Sino-Japanese relations. Particularly, it focuses on China's decision to oppose Japan's entry into the UN Security Council as a permanent member in 2005, an opposition that continues today. Again using hundreds of articles in the official and mainstream Chinese media, it shows that the dominant goal of victimhood explains China's hostility to the idea of Japan as a permanent member of the Security Council.

This book makes three important contributions to the field of international relations. First, it offers a way to systematically treat history, specifically colonial history, as an explanatory variable. Colonialism was such a curious and hugely influential phenomenon. While the motivations of colonizers and the brutal effects of colonialism have been widely discussed, less attention has been paid to why and how this past continues to matter to the countries that have undergone it as they negotiate international society.

Second, it offers a new method of categorizing states that have very different power structures and regimes. International relations usually focuses on states that "matter" (based on their significant material capabilities), or are "successful" (based on their ability to impose or break norms).[13] These are usually Western states. The behavior of developing nations is often overlooked. Even when they are taken into account, they are analyzed in contrast to developed nations on the basis of their disparities in economic or military power.[14] But a large category of states claim that their past matters very much to them and have an ideology of victimhood, and this leads them to behave in ways that liberals or realists do not necessarily predict. Thus the transformative historical event of colonialism can be used as a tool to categorize these states and explain key variations in their foreign policy.

Third, it uses a new lens to look at two important examples from this category of states—India and China. Because these are rising powers, the dominant lens used to analyze and contrast their behavior has been state security. But as this book shows, not only does this exclude a recognition of the past that the states themselves emphasize is so important, but also it does not allow for the simple fact that in very important cases, their foreign policy behavior is not consistent with security explanations. When these countries feel that their sovereignty is threatened, non-negotiable borders are at stake, or their prestige might suffer, PII better explains their behavior than traditional approaches that emphasize security only.

In India and China, the colonial history of each is deeply rooted in their culture, in their education and in their politics. Children, growing up, hear stories or study in school anecdotes and "facts" about their colonial history[15]—the Bengal famine in India that killed millions was caused by British policies,[16] the British chopped off the thumbs of weavers in India so they would be unable to produce textiles that were higher quality than British manufactured goods,[17] Indian and Chinese historical artifacts were looted and sent out of the country, "no dogs or Chinese" and "no dogs or Indians" signs were posted in the parks and clubs,[18] the Japanese massacred, pillaged and raped in Nanjing, and many others. This emphasis on their colonial past means that any discourse of "engaging" or "managing" these two powers needs to move beyond simple security explanations of their behavior and include their sense of victimhood and its corollary, a sense of entitlement and recovery in international relations.

Whether one believes the brutality of colonialism and the suffering of these countries is exaggerated or not, and certainly at times it is, what is important is that these countries believe it and respond accordingly. That is the fundamental basis of this book.

1

Trauma, Colonialism and Post-Imperial Ideology

Introduction

This chapter explores two new concepts. First, through the exploration of trauma theory, it argues that the transformative historical event of colonialism in India and China can be classified as a collective trauma. Second, by changing the lens through which colonialism in India and China is viewed, it is possible to identify a "post-imperial ideology," or PII.[1] PII is rooted in a mentality of victimhood and is an essential component of both India's and China's national identity and, therefore, their international outlook. As subsequent chapters show, PII can then be used as an independent variable to analyze important foreign policy decisions taken by these rising powers.

Even a cursory examination of international politics demonstrates the ubiquity of colonialism and its effects. Despite the dismantling of the colonial empire more than half a century ago, the legacy of colonialism has played out in dramatic and tragic fashion. From the ongoing war in Iraq to the persistence of the Israel-Palestine violence to the territorial dispute in Kashmir, many continuing conflicts today are heavily influenced by the vagaries of colonialism.[2] The impact of colonialism on economics, history, politics and culture has been widely discussed and dissected, and details of its brutality and exploitative nature have been explored. Yet, surprisingly, given the amount of ink devoted to the subject, there has been little systematic treatment of colonialism. This book argues that colonialism can be seen in two lights simultaneously. It is both a collective historical trauma and a causal variable that continues to influence the international outlook of states decades after decolonization. Viewing colonialism in such ways is new to the study of international politics.[3]

The concept of colonialism as trauma is particularly true for India and China, which attach immense significance to their colonial past. India and China underwent very different experiences of colonialism. Yet the "intensity" of this experience was similar for the two countries—both India and China regarded and responded to colonialism as a collective historical trauma. As a result they have a self-definition of victimhood. By this I mean, they believed themselves to have been victimized, and, as a consequence, adopt the position of victim in their responses to international issues even today.

As such they have a dominant goal of victimhood: the desire to be recognized and empathized with in the international system as a victim. The goal of victimhood carries with it a corresponding sense of entitlement that manifests itself in two subordinate goals: maximizing territorial sovereignty and maximizing status. The dominant goal of victimhood driving the subordinate goals of territorial sovereignty and status constitute a "post-imperial ideology" (PII) that influences international behavior. While PII affects a range of state behavior, its influence is most apparent when states perceive threats to sovereignty, when borders viewed as non-negotiable are contested or when a state's international prestige is jeopardized.

Particularly, it does so by leading states traumatized by colonialism to first, adopt the position of victim and cast other states as victimizers; second, justify their actions or stances through a discourse invoking oppression and discrimination; third, adopt strict concepts of the inviolability of borders; and fourth, have a sensitivity to loss of face and a desire to regain "lost" status. Any analysis of India and China as rising powers is incomplete without taking into account this past that continues to shape their international outlook.

This chapter first discusses the impact of colonialism as a transformative historical event before briefly detailing the different experiences of colonialism in India and China. It then moves on to discuss trauma theory and how colonialism in India and China can be viewed through the theoretical framework of collective historical trauma. Finally, it discusses the three goals of PII and their emergence in state discourse and behavior after decolonization.

Imperialism and Colonialism: A Transformative Historical Event

I define a transformative historical event as *an event which can either lead to the creation of a new state or can reshape an existing state by altering key political and military institutions and the ideology thereof, that are intrinsic to the state.* The decolonization of Asia and Africa in the 1940s, 50s and 60s led to the creation of new states as well as the complete transformation of existing states by changing their pre-colonial political and military institutions. Post-colonial states such as modern India and China were, as I will discuss, radically different from their pre-colonial form. In this way, imperialism and colonialism were a transformative historical event.[4]

Imperialism and colonialism are terms that are often used interchangeably. The concept of imperialism has been elaborately defined by writers: from Hobson and Lenin, who viewed it as a metropolitan initiative driven by the profit motive, to Doyle, who termed it "a relationship, formal or informal, in which one state controls the effective political sovereignty of another political society . . . [that] can be achieved by force, by political collaboration, by economic, social, or cultural dependence."[5] Colonialism, a more difficult concept, is seen as a subset or outcome of imperialism.[6] My theory refers to the transformative historical event of modern "imperialism and colonialism" taken together as a whole, and is concerned with extractive colonialism rather than settler colonialism. Extractive colonialism transformed pre-colonial societies, while settler colonialism often displaced them with populations from elsewhere.

Under extractive colonialism the colonizing power established an "extractive state" whose purpose was to shift the resources of the colony to the colonizer, often with few to no protections for the native populace against abuse by the colonial authority.[7] Extractive colonialism came in different forms in different societies, but elements of these institutions had a striking resonance for all countries that experienced them: external political dominance, economic exploitation, denial of rights, and suppression of cultural and ethnic pride.

The demise of extractive colonialism was directly linked with a radical change in the normative structure of the international system.[8] The colonial system was severely criticized and, as Jackson puts it, "lost its moral force" in the face of the ascendant "normative idea of self-determination."[9] Crawford similarly argues that it became unacceptable for states to keep colonies because it was "wrong to deny nations and individuals political self-determination."[10] Not only was independence now a basic right, but colonialism was "an absolute wrong"—"an injury to the dignity and autonomy of those peoples and a vehicle for their economic exploitation and political oppression."[11] Through textbooks, cultural and social discourse, international conferences like Bandung in 1955, biographies and newspapers, the newly independent states would view their experience of extractive colonialism through a prism of victimization, suffering and endurance. Effectively, as I will discuss, this experience was a collective trauma.

It is important to discuss briefly the history of colonialism in India and China prior to demonstrating that both states encountered similarly "intense" experiences of colonialism that met the standard of collective trauma.

A History of Colonialism in India and China

For modern India and modern China, there was and is a strong distinction made between the previous rule of the country by various dynasties, some of which had external origins, and the later influx of colonial powers from the West and Japan.

In India, the pre-British dynasties of the Delhi Sultanate and the Mughals were not termed "colonizers." Rather, the history of India up until the British period, and the encounter with the English East India Company,[12] is one of assimilation of and accommodation with the waves of foreigners landing on its shores. There was no "clear distinguishing line between Islamic civilization and the pre existing corpus of 'Hindu tradition,'" and, in fact, "creative Indo-Islamic accommodations of difference were worked out at various levels of society and culture."[13] Even the first Europeans to set up a base in India—the Portuguese led by Vasco da Gama in 1498—"settled within the structure and were, in a way, swallowed by it."[14] What the advent of British rule brought was a clear line drawn between the natives and the outsiders, and the need for the country to adapt to the modern world.

The transition to colonial rule in India took place in the mid-18th century with the gradual dismantling of the Mughal empire. The English East India Company upon arrival in the seventeenth century was a petitioner that sought the right to trade from the Mughals and obtained permission to do so from Emperor Jahangir in 1619. In 1757, the Company took the first major step toward the establishment of British colonial rule in India by defeating Siraj-ud-daula, the *nawab* of Bengal, at the Battle of Plassey. The Company, whose political and military power had hitherto been limited to a few factory forts in coastal areas, had been competing for turf with the French East India Company. The *nawab* had objected to the Company's building fortifications in Calcutta to ward off the French. The victorious British acquired vast rights to operate in the *nawab*'s domain, concessions that enriched Company coffers and prepared them for the Battle of Buxar in 1764, where they decisively defeated the combined armies of the *nawabs* of Bengal and Awadh and the Mughal emperor. This victory forced the Mughal emperor to grant them the *diwani,* the right to collect the revenues of Bengal.

The East India Company's new financial and military strength gradually

FIG. I.I. Capture of the King of Delhi, 1857–58. Source: Anne S. K. Brown Military Collection, Brown University Library.

enabled them to extend their rule over the subcontinent. In 1857, a widespread revolt against British rule erupted. When it was crushed by the British at great expense, the Crown decided to dissolve the East India Company and instead rule India directly through a Viceroy governing as the Crown representative, a system that would remain until independence and partition in 1947.

Post-1857 saw the rise of organized anti-colonial nationalism motivated by the belief that a hundred years of British rule had already, economically and politically, crippled the country and, thus, demanded a movement to regain India's sense of worth. The early strands of the nationalist movement eventually gave way to Gandhian tactics and the dominance of the Indian National Congress.

In Chinese historiography, too, the beginning of the modern period is marked by a clear border between the previous conquests of China and the influx of the Western powers and Japan (bitterly termed *yang guize,* or foreign devils) into China. Paine states that history books present the modern period as "beginning with the defeats in the Opium Wars followed by a century of uninterrupted concessions and humiliations before foreigners."[15] It has been sug-

FIG. 1.2. The Signing and Sealing of the Treaty of Nanking, F. G. Moon, 1846. Source: Anne S. K. Brown Military Collection, Brown University Library.

gested that the Qing were in fact colonizers. The Qing were, after all, Manchus who conquered the existing Han Chinese population, and proceeded to ban Han Chinese from holding high government posts or intermarrying with the Manchus. Dissenters counter that the Qing carefully upheld Confucian structures and Chinese traditions in order to emphasize their claim to "the Mandate of Heaven" (*tian ming*). Paine remarks, "[M]odern history marks the first time that China had ever been completely unable to sinicize the outsiders but had instead been forced, however reluctantly and painfully, to adapt to the world beyond China."[16] Arguments about the nativization of the Qing notwithstanding, there is no doubt that the Chinese nationalist movement, though critical of the corruption of the dynasty, not only embraced the territorial boundaries and legacy of the Qing but also had an anti-foreign powers doctrine at its core. This trend continued even when the Guomindang was replaced by the Chinese Communist Party (CCP). Thus, the Chinese see the modern history of colonialism in China as two-pronged—the carving up of Qing China into foreign spheres of influence by Western powers and Japan (1842–1905), and the later domination by Japan during World War II (1931–45). Both phases of imperialism have strong resonance for the Chinese and are collectively remembered as the "century of humiliation" (*bainian guochi*). Indeed, Mao referred to China during this period as *ban zhimin di,* or, a semi-colony.

The insulated Chinese empire's first brush with European powers occurred through Portugal's merchants in the Far East in the early sixteenth century. "The Chinese did not realize the significance of the Portuguese arrival, but it initiated a process that would end by destroying the Empire and engulfing China."[17] The first British trading ships entered Guangzhou (Canton) circa 1637, and between 1685 and 1759 the English and other Europeans traded at several places along the Chinese coast, including Xiamen, Fuzhou and Ningbo.[18] After 1759, Guangzhou was designated the sole port open to Europeans. The isolation of the Qing empire from the realities of the outside world meant that the trade with the British and Dutch East India companies was still "nominally conducted as though it were a boon granted to tributary states."[19]

Ultimately, opium imports from India to China led to a crisis. Opium was produced in India and sold at auction under official British auspices and then taken to China by private British traders licensed by the East India Company. Opium sales at Guangzhou paid for the substantial tea trade to London. The reversal of the balance of trade and the drain of silver from China to pay for increasing imports of opium, combined with the societal effects of opium addiction, alarmed the Qing.[20] The ensuing clash resulted in the Opium War of 1839–42, and China's defeat in that conflict secured Qing agreement to the

Treaty of Nanjing in 1842, substantially increasing British access to Chinese ports.

This was only the beginning of the encroachment that transformed the empire's relationship with the West. A second war fought by the British and the French against the Qing secured them treaties at Tianjin in 1858 that allowed Western ministers to "live at Peking within a context of equality as understood in Western diplomatic practice."[21] In October 1860 the allies captured Peking, an event that dismantled the traditional tribute system and replaced it with the "unequal treaty system." Although China's treaties with Britain, the United States, France and Russia were signed as between equal sovereign powers, they were blatantly lopsided. "China was placed against her will in a weaker position open to the inroads of Western commerce and its attendant culture."[22]

China suffered from 1870 to 1905 as a consequence of great power rivalries among the industrializing states. China served either as an arena of competition or a potential source of revenue that could be utilized elsewhere. Russia, France, Germany, Great Britain and Japan all invaded Qing territory over this period. China's defeat by Japan and the signing of the Treaty of Shimonoseki in 1895 forced the Qing to cede Taiwan to the Japanese. This episode was particularly bitter, with a former vassal state defeating a country that considered itself the center of civilization. China's resentment toward Japan originated with this episode, though subsequent events would magnify China's grievances. The Qing dynasty survived till 1912 only because there was no alternative regime to replace it. Organized Chinese nationalism burgeoned in 1905 when Sun Yatsen became the head of the Revolutionary League at a meeting of Chinese students in Tokyo.

Japan's occupation of Manchuria marked the beginning of the second phase of imperialism (1931–45). By 1932, the Japanese had conquered the whole of Manchuria and set up a Japanese-controlled state called Manchukuo. By the end of 1938, the Japanese controlled almost all of east and southeastern China, encompassing some 1.5 million square kilometers of land and a population of more than 170 million. They set up a puppet government in Peking and Nanjing and announced the establishment of "the new order in East Asia."[23] Japan's aggression strengthened Chinese nationalism and temporarily united the Guomindang and the Chinese Communist Party in a patchy alliance.

The preoccupation with colonial heritage, manifest in anti-colonial nationalism and carried into the post-imperial era through school and college textbooks and in political and social discourse, is similar in these two countries despite their contrasting patterns of colonization—the complete colonization of India for two hundred years and the piecemeal colonization of China over a similar timeframe. The "intensity" of the colonial experience in each country is comparable because in each case the experience was a collective historical and cultural trauma. That history in both countries is constructed and subjective—conspicuously evident in the Chinese emphasis on the Western and Japanese intrusion into China while omitting any reference to the Manchu Qing dynasty—does not change the social reality created from the colonial experience. The fact that it is perceived as a collective trauma makes it a collective trauma. Indeed, as one can show through the framework of trauma theory, trauma is often subjective rather than objective.

An Exploration of Trauma

The core of anti-colonial nationalism that emerged in colonized states was an emphasis on the sufferings and injuries of colonial rule and the search for redress. Even after independence, these states continued to give the utmost importance to the wrongs they had suffered and the quest for restitution. The high-profile and significant Afro-Asian Bandung Conference of 1955 was an explicit portrayal of the victimization and suffering these states believed they had undergone. Not only was Bandung a collective Afro-Asian stance against imperialism and colonialism, but speech after speech detailed past and continued humiliations and exploitation. The prime minister of Indonesia, Ali Sastroamidjojo, in his welcome speech to the delegates, bitterly declared:

> Next to colonialism we meet racialism as an important source of tension. Racialism in fact is often, if not always, an aspect of colonialism based on feelings of superiority of the dominating group. Discrimination, however, based on differences of color is contrary to the fundamental human rights, to the essential quality of mankind as rightly expressed in the Charter of the United Nations. In today's world we are still a long way off from this equality and respect for human rights . . . . Another and very serious source of tension is the low standard of living in practically all Asian and African countries. For centuries out countries have poured a never-ending stream of profits into the dominating countries, but we ourselves stayed poor and underdeveloped.[24]

As Sastroamidjojo's statement shows, even after decolonization, these states felt themselves to be victims in international society. In order to examine how this narrative of suffering and the language of victimhood is consistent with trauma, it is necessary to delve into the massive theoretical literature on trauma. Our starting point must be with the very definition of the concept. What constitutes trauma? And more specifically, what is collective trauma?

What Is Trauma?

The etymology of the word "trauma" can be traced to the Greek word for "wound." A cursory glance at newspapers suggests that the word in various forms is used frequently and casually—"traumatized," "traumatic," "trauma" are words used in news stories that range from covering the war in Afghanistan to Michael Jackson's death. The word is part of our daily lexicon. Not surprisingly, there is a wide-ranging body of literature on trauma drawn primarily from psychology but also from history, sociology, anthropology and literary studies. This book incorporates those findings into the study of international politics.

Trauma theory has grappled with many (non-exclusive) types of trauma—historical, cultural, inter-generational, social, and individual—from many sources—rape, war, genocide, and abuse, to name a few. The unstated common element is that trauma is almost invariably related to implied or actual violence. As Kirmayer et al. point out, "[T]rauma has become a keyword through which clinicians and scholars from many disciplines approach the experience of violence and its aftermath . . . .[It] can be seen at once as a sociopolitical event, a psychophysiological process, a physical and emotional experience, and a narrative theme in explanations of individual and social suffering."[25]

Thus, "[T]raumatic events generally involve threats to life or bodily integrity or a close personal encounter with violence and death . . . . [T]he common denominator of psychological trauma is a feeling of 'intense fear, helplessness, loss of control, and threat of annihilation.'"[26] Trauma is a "shock that is deemed emotional and substantially damages, over a long time period, the psychological development of the victim, often leading to neurosis."[27] It is a "nonordinary human experience that may lead to post-traumatic stress disorder (PTSD), and which would be distressing to most people, such as serious harm or threat to self, spouse, children, close relatives or friends; witnessing a serious accident or violence against another person, who, as a result is either killed or seriously injured; or having one's home or community suddenly destroyed."[28] The clinical classification most commonly associated with the experience of trauma, particularly individual trauma, is PTSD, and there is an extraordinary amount of work in psychology on the subject. However, trauma can cover "a much larger and more ambiguous terrain than the construct of PTSD would suggest, contributing to individual and collective identities and the politics of memory."[29]

The theoretical work on cultural and historical trauma falls into this larger terrain, and it is primarily concerned with the social rather than the individual. While the more individualistic biological dimension of trauma is important, a more encompassing way to understand it is as a "socially positioned process" rather than a mere biological state. In other words, the entrenchment of trauma in social, cultural and political relations is as important as the scientific research on the biology of fear, arousal or pain.[30] Trauma theory entered lay dialogue as well as systematic research as a result of efforts to understand the "shell shock" that affected the veterans of World War I, eventually incorporating other events including the Holocaust, other episodes of genocide and the atomic bombing of Hiroshima.[31]

The effects of trauma on a whole community are complex and controversial. Understanding these effects quickly requires confronting questions of memory and particularly transgenerational memory, as well as the nature of trauma's impact on communal life, core social institutions and cultural values. The phrase "historical trauma" has often been used in relation with research on indigenous peoples, where it has provided a link between the impact of colonization and forced assimilation to current social and mental health problems.[32] At a very basic level, the presence of historical trauma implies a historical event that meets the standard of a trauma, which in turn generated individual and collective responses that have been transferred across generations. A more specific conceptualization of historical trauma focuses on cultural or social trauma.

Cultural trauma "occurs when members of a collectivity feel they have been subjected to a horrendous event that leaves indelible marks upon their group consciousness, marking their memories forever and changing their future identity in fundamental and irrevocable ways."[33] Certain attributes need to be present for a historical event to classify as cultural trauma—the memory "must be remembered or made to be remembered"; the memory must be made "culturally relevant" by "obliterating, damaging or rendering problematic something sacred like a value; the memory must be "negative."[34] Examples given of cultural trauma range from specific historical events such as the regicide of Louis XVI in the French Revolution to broader experiences such as slavery and the Protestant Reformation,[35] and more recent events such as 9/11[36] and the Bali bombings of 2002.[37] The defining element of social trauma is that it "massively disrupts organized social life" and the "affected arenas are society's social structures" such as economic, legal and political institutions.[38] Disease, famine and war all constitute social trauma, while more specific events such as the Great Depression can be regarded as both socially and culturally traumatic.[39]

How Do We Remember the Past?: Trauma and Memory

Any discussion of trauma needs to address the question of how that trauma is remembered. Historical trauma is therefore intimately linked to theories of memory and, particularly, collective memory. Memory has been broadly defined as "our capacity for acquiring, retaining, and using information."[40] Daniel Schacter calls memory "fragile power."[41] Both implicit ("memory without awareness") and explicit memory ("conscious recollection")[42] are crucial for understanding why and how the past influences the present. Researchers have taken the importance of memories to individuals a step further and applied it to a collective psyche. For example, by examining Soviet-educated and post-Soviet subjects' accounts of World War II, it has been shown that their perspective is distinct from the usual perspectives held by people from other countries.[43] Collective memory is simply "public recollection—the act of gathering bits and pieces of the past and joining them together in public."[44] Collective memory is ultimately the linking mechanism between past trauma and any ongoing response to that trauma.

There are several points that are important when exploring the connection between trauma and memory. Memory is about behavior as well as thought. Memory is "reconstructive," or about the "reassembly of encoded elements of experience that are distributed throughout the brain." Memory can be focused, since "intense emotion enhances memory for the central aspects of stressful experiences." Memory need not be objective, since people are able to believe that they underwent stressful events that never took place. Finally, memory need not come from personal experience alone: people that did not witness trauma directly, but have heard it recalled by others, can develop a response like PTSD to that trauma.[45]

The last two points about memory and trauma are particularly important— people can believe events occurred that did not happen, as well as believe altered accounts of those events, and people can experience trauma secondhand. It has even been pointed out that three memory-related variables may feature in any definition of trauma—"an objectively defined event, the person's subjective interpretation of its meaning, and the person's emotional reaction to it."[46] There is consequently a distinction between history and traumatic memory, between objective and subjective history.

Some would say that the collective memory approach is naturally subjective, as it is not possible to have a unified, detailed and universally accepted version of events.[47] Rather, it is drawn from "the 'stock of stories' that exist in [our] socio-cultural context" and its function is to provide a "usable past."[48] *But objectivity versus subjectivity does not diminish the significance of the trauma or the response to that trauma.* Myth-making (a "historically problematic narrative explaining collective identity") and mimesis ("rituals" that identify with past "peoples and tropes"), for example, can be an integral part of making sense of past trauma.[49] Young, in fact, asserts that "trauma's meaning" can only be completely understood "retrospectively" because it is initially too unexpected and therefore "incomprehensible." He gives the example of the collective memory of the Holocaust, which only became *the Holocaust* in the 1960s with the Eichmann trial in Jerusalem. Prior to that, although there was information about death camps, it did not exist as a "discrete, knowable trauma."[50]

The discussion of trauma and collective memory, objectivity versus subjectivity, throws up two last crucial questions before we turn to examine extractive colonialism in India and China as a collective trauma. *Who remembers? And why do they remember?*

Who Remembers the Past and Why?

The question of whose collective memory of trauma has three important implications—first, trauma is socially mediated; second, there exists some agent that engages in collective remembrance; and last, there is intergenerational transmission of that trauma.

An event is not collectively traumatic unless and until it is socially mediated.[51] This means there is agency at work, in which individuals remember the event(s) as trauma and transmit that memory to a larger community.

> Individuals in society learn, but their learning has sufficient overlap for us to be able to speak metaphorically of social learning. It follows that for two or more individuals to hold the same memory, even if they have experienced the same event, means only that there is sufficient overlap between their memory traces. For this overlap to become a social phenomenon it must be expressed and shared. In this sense, and in this sense alone, can one speak, again metaphorically, of "collective memory." . . . As long as there are individuals using . . . [memory] aids, whether internally or externally in order to rehearse their memories, then the process of remembrance is alive.[52]

The agents of the trauma recollection process have also been called what Weber termed "carrier groups."[53] These groups have ideational and material interests, are positioned in key places in the social structure and are talented at clearly expressing their claims.[54]

One may think that these agents are naturally elites because their social positioning is such that they can strongly influence and even manipulate collective memory. However, while agents certainly can be elites, they are not confined to the elite. Research has shown that "memory work" is often carried on spontaneously within civil society, including denigrated and marginalized classes, especially after events that are particularly meaningful. "Agency in the constitution of social learning about the past is crucial but it operates from below, not only from above."[55]

Collective memory of trauma has also been shown to be inter-generational. Studies show that remembrance of trauma has been passed down to the next generation channeled through survivors and survivor groups.[56] Research has focused on the inter-generational effects of the Holocaust, "perhaps the most dramatic example of the extreme victimization of a specific group."[57] Children and grandchildren can serve as re-activators of trauma, while in Israel the phrase "second generation" is commonly used to describe the grown children of Holocaust survivors.[58] Studies have also shown the traumatic effect of dependency and colonialism on Aborigines and Native Americans, and the subsequent carry-over of that trauma through several generations.[59]

The question of *who* remembers trauma goes some way toward answering *why* it is remembered. As I mentioned earlier, carrier groups have both ideational and material interests. Thus, survivors of the Holocaust, for example, had incentives ranging from finding and/or mourning lost family members, engaging in catharsis of personal horrors, protecting future generations and recovering stolen personal possessions and property. A trauma suffered implies a disruption of social order. Its remembrance can become an important element of a collective identity and at its most extreme can even define a collective identity. Also, Alexander points out that it is "by constructing cultural traumas that social groups, national societies, and sometimes even entire civilizations cognitively identify the existence and source of human suffering."[60]

We have now discussed what trauma is, how it is transmitted, who can transmit and why they do so. The issue before us now is how this can be extrapolated to the transformative historical event of colonialism. And importantly, ascertaining whether and how the transformative historical event of extractive colonialism in India and China was a collective trauma.

Scars of Empire: The Collective Trauma of Colonialism
in India and China

The transformative experience of colonialism in India and China can be reframed through the lens of trauma. The narrative of suffering and the language of victimhood that emerged from the colonial experience are consistent with the theoretical framework of collective trauma.

Collective trauma implies a disruption of social order. Arthur Neal's work extrapolates the anguish and social disorder of collective trauma to the nation. He discusses how national trauma with its elements of fear and vulnerability "permanently changed" the United States.[61] Using examples such as the

Japanese surprise attack on Pearl Harbor, the Cuban missile crisis and 9/11, he argues that these traumas became entrenched in collective memory that then served as reference points used to situate future occurrences.[62] Neal's examples are primarily instantaneous events that delivered rapid shocks, and generally have been accepted as illustrative of collective trauma.

Consider then, the grim history of colonialism usually encompassing a century or more of violence and political, economic and cultural exploitation. Its very essence was domination and subordination. The phenomenon of colonialism was not encapsulated by a single instantaneous event but rather by many such events that would eventually become the focus of anti-colonial nationalism and mass uprisings. After decolonization, these events would be entrenched in history textbooks and national discourse as the symbol and a reminder of repressive colonial rule. In both India and China, despite the contrasting patterns of colonization, colonialism was cast as a collective historical trauma.

In India, the first glimmer of a backlash against the oppression of colonial rule was with the Revolt of 1857. However, while the revolt was sparked by general discontent against the British East India Company and its policies, its expression was fractured with competing interests.[63] There was no clear identification of anti-British grievances. After its suppression, Company *Raj* gave way to Crown *Raj*. Competing strands of Indian nationalism began to emerge. Among these, one of the earliest conclusions reached by Indian nationalists—even those seeking reform of British rule rather than independence—was a direct link between British economic exploitation and India's poverty.[64]

Dadabhai Naoroji, one of India's most famous early nationalists and leaders, painfully expostulated a "drain of wealth" from India to Britain through speeches and articles that had great resonance with the nationalist movement. In a speech to the British government, he declared,

> The way you secure life and property is by protecting it from open violence by anybody else, taking care that you yourselves should take away that property. . . . Look at the millions that are suffering day by day, year after year, even in years of good harvest. Seven-eighths or nine-tenths of the people do not know what it is to have a full meal in a day. . . . It is the Englishmen that go out to India that are in a sense the cause of these miseries. They go to India to benefit themselves. . . . The "bleeding" which is carried on means impoverishment to us—the poorest people on the face of the earth—with all the dire, calamitous consequences of famines, pestilence and destruction. It is but the result of what you claim as the best thing that you have conferred upon us—security of life and property—starvation, as I have told you . . . and something worse, in addition to the "bleeding" that is carried on by the officials of a system of government. . . . You inflict injustice upon us in a manner most dishonourable and discreditable to yourselves.[65]

In another letter sent to the Welby Commission, Naoroji could barely contain his anger:

> The British Empire in India is built up entirely with the money of India, and in great measure, by the blood of India. . . . In reality there are two Indias—one the prosperous, the other poverty-stricken. The prosperous India is the India of the British and other foreigners. They exploit India as officials, non-officials, capitalists, in a variety of ways, and carry away enormous wealth to their own country. The second India is the India of the Indians—the poverty-stricken India. This India "bled" and exploited in every way of their wealth, of their services, of their land, labour, and all resources by the foreigners, helpless and voiceless, governed by the arbitrary law and arguments of force, and with injustice and unrighteousness—this India of the Indians becomes the poorest country in the world, after one hundred and fifty years of British rule. The greater the drain, the greater the impoverishment, resulting in all the scourges of war, famine and pestilence.[66]

In addition to the grievance of economic exploitation by the British, Indian nationalists were also acutely sensitive to political and cultural humiliation and subjugation. The British were on a "civilizing mission," and the dispensation of education and governance, and the maintenance of order were all from an untouchable position of superiority vis-à-vis the natives. There was no or limited franchise, no opportunity of advancement to the high echelons of government, segregated political and social institutions to maintain strict social boundaries, and the promotion of the English language at the expense of the vernacular.[67] It was, to Indian nationalists, the rule of "the slave-master over the slave."[68]

In addition to systemic injustices, colonialism in India was accompanied by incidents of shocking violence that would be etched in collective memory long after Indian independence in 1947. The Jallianwala Bagh massacre, immortalized in the hugely popular movie *Gandhi*, was one such event. In 1919, British Indian army soldiers under the command of Brigadier General Reginald Dyer opened fire on a peaceful gathering of men, women, and children in Jallianwala Bagh ("park") in Amritsar. The movie dwelt on the drama and bloodshed, showing how Dyer ordered one exit to the park be closed and the soldiers to reload and fire until they ran out of ammunition.

In China too, the history of colonialism, although characterized by "multiple imperialisms that competed and cooperated,"[69] rather than continuous rule by one colonial power, was seen as one of political and economic exploitation, accompanied by episodes of violence and brutality. Modern nationalist accounts of the evils of colonialism in China detailed the "aggressive wars and economic plunder" that the weak Qing government failed to stop.[70] These included humiliating unequal treaties imposed on China by the Western powers and Japan that, among other harms, required the payment of huge indemnities, forced access to Chinese ports, seized control over lucrative industries such as mining and railways, asserted jurisdiction over large swaths of formerly Qing territories, and demanded special treatment of Christian missionaries.[71] Hu's classic account of colonialism in China bitterly points out, "Britain launched the [opium] war to expand its economic sway by using armed force to enslave the Chinese people. . . . [T]he British forces when they landed on Chinese soil massacred and looted in the usual fashion of colonial wars. Thus a widespread bitter enmity of the Chinese people toward the 'foreign devils' was aroused for the first time."[72]

As in colonial India, Chinese resentment and "enmity" was further stoked by institutionalized discrimination and incidents of violence in addition to loss of political and economic control. Injustice and control were, in fact, related. Colonial settlers like the British knew that the support of the British government would wane unless they demonstrated a commitment to British institutions and social practices. The "mock Raj" instituted some of the same social boundaries the British had adopted in India, such as separate clubs, parks, schools, and residences.[73] The desire to maintain British "ethnicity" often went hand in hand with a dehumanization of the Chinese and little regard for their person or life. Routine violence toward the natives was common enough to enter the vernacular slang—eating *waiguo huotai* ("foreign ham") implied the frequent kicks aimed at rickshaw pullers by foreign passengers. Similarly, the 1936 acquittal of a sergeant in the murder of a sick Chinese beggar was and remains infamous.[74]

Social humiliations aside, there were also large-scale incidents of violence, notably the Tianjin Incident of 1870, in which the French opened fire on Qing officials and anti-French demonstrators, the looting and brutal massacres in response to the Boxer uprising (often called the Chinese "Indian mutiny"),[75] and the most notorious of all, the Nanjing Massacre. The latter is considered one of the most painful episodes in the Chinese colonial experience. Post-colonialism, Chinese literature (Ah Long's *Nanjing*, Ye Zhaoyan's *Nanjing 1937: A Love Story*), film (state-produced *The Massacre of Nanjing, Actual Record of the Nanjing Massacre, Eyewitness to History*) and non-fictional books (Iris Chang's *The Rape of Nanjing*) have dwelt on the death toll, brutality, mutilation, torture and rape of Nanjing residents by the Japanese.

Nationalists articulated grievances against colonial rule that became a part of the collective memory of colonialism in India and China. Any school-going child growing up in India has heard of Jallianwala Bagh, as well as other cruelties of British rule such as the chopping off of the thumbs of the Bengal weavers to make British textiles more competitive, just as Chinese students know of the Nanjing Massacre, the encroachment of foreign missionaries, and parks labeled "no dogs or Chinese." The narrative of colonialism in both countries, regarded as transformative and characterized by oppression, humiliation and violence, is consistent with trauma theorists' definitions of cultural and social trauma.

By this I mean, nationalist accounts, both during and after decolonization, reflected the feelings of a collective subjected to a horrendous event that was a massive disruption to organized social structures and, as a result, changed future social identities. As for the question of who transmits this colonial past as trauma, I had earlier outlined the role of agents that remember events as trauma. In India and China, this role was carried out by early and later nationalists as well as state-sponsored school and college textbooks, media,[76] and, in the case of India, through the political discourse of politicians who aspired to the anti-colonial nationalist legacy.

Was this remembrance of trauma entirely objective? Almost certainly not. While there are general agreements about the facts of colonialism, many important events such as the Nanjing Massacre as well as theories such as the "drain of wealth" are disputed. But this does not alter or diminish the trauma. Social actors perceived colonialism as traumatic, an indisputable injustice and "wrong," and hence it was those things.

Today the notion of colonialism as a "wrong" is accepted as intuitively right and proper, but in the mid-twentieth century it was an explosively radical idea. It overturned the established notions of rights to sovereign statehood, international legitimacy, and the "responsibilities" of "civilized" states.[77] India and China emerged in the international system in a new avatar with hotly contested post-imperial boundaries, anti-colonial nationalism and a burning desire to regain a sense of worth by making a mark in the new order. Thus, shaped by their colonial trauma, which ended only after their struggles to gain the moral right to self-determination, in a world for which that right had become a primary value, they had a fundamentally different outlook than states that had not undergone such experiences. Even after decolonization, these states continued to give the utmost importance to the wrongs they had suffered and the quest for restitution for those past ills. This outlook, transmitted and institutionalized through collective memory, shaped a self-definition of victimhood. This self-definition would prove integral to their new national identities. It would manifest itself as post-imperial ideology, or PII.

PII in India and China

India and China perceived the transformative historical event of colonialism as a form of collective trauma. PII represents the identity shift that resulted from that trauma. It is composed of the dominant goal of victimhood driving the subordinate goals of territorial sovereignty and status. PII strongly influences India's and China's international behavior in three notable circumstances: when they perceive a threat to sovereignty, when borders they consider traditional are at stake or when their national prestige is impugned.

In such circumstances, several behaviors tend to manifest themselves in several discrete ways. First, PII states adopt the position of victim and cast those with which it is interacting as victimizers. Second, these states often justify their actions or international stances by invoking a discourse of oppression and discrimination. Third, PII states adhere to strict concepts of the inviolability of their borders, often related to a desire to regain "lost" territories that they believe were intruded upon by colonialism. Fourth, they have an acute sensitivity to any perceived loss of face that corresponds with a similar desire to regain "lost" status.

The dominant goal of PII is victimhood. India's and China's traumatic colonial experience generated national beliefs involving a strong sense of victimization and suffering that continued after decolonization. Mark Ashley's work suggests that nationalists employ a narrative of national victimization that perceives the Self as worthy and superior to other cultures, identifies and denigrates an external Other who is inferior to the Self, and contains a discourse of real or invented suffering.[78] While India and China do not necessarily hold an image of themselves as superior to other cultural communities (although they often do), they do identify "others" as victimizers who have caused them suffering or harm. While the colonizing powers receive considerable blame for their past exploitation, new victimizers not directly related to colonial-era exploitation can also play the role of the "other" in the evolving post-colonial narrative.

In India, various strands of nationalism emerged in response to British colonial rule. Each strand, whether moderate, extremist or Gandhian, offered different methods and institutions to cope with the colonial administration. Distinct in their approaches—from violence to peaceful reform to civil disobedience—they were united, as mentioned earlier, by a strong consciousness of suffering inflicted under British rule. This consciousness remains. Although the contours of nationalism—from Congress-led socialist to the Bharatiya Janata Party's Hindu chauvinist—have changed, the consciousness of past exploitation and continued mistreatment is enduring.

The sense of injury is wide-ranging and pervasive. It encompasses grievances from the past and slights in the present, with the victimizer a changing variable. Whether it is the belief that India's economic problems and poverty stemmed from the "drain of wealth" during the colonial era, or that its lost artifacts—such as the Kohinoor diamond, which currently graces the crown of the British monarchy—were plundered, or that it lost a large part of its territory, Pakistan, as a result of Britain's divide-and-rule policies, or that the United States and other developed powers conspire against India's industrial development by demanding that it rein in its industrial pollution while refusing to share their green technology, or even that the United States ignores Pakistani funding of cross-border terrorist groups in Kashmir, India is convinced that it is a victim and that international society should acknowledge it as such.

From time to time this explodes into very specific requests for acknowledgment, such as the 1997 furor over Queen Elizabeth's visit to India, when public opinion demanded she apologize for the Jallianwala Bagh incident or the diplomatic fracas in 2004, when the Indian media indignantly reported that Defence Minister George Fernandes had been strip-searched twice at a U.S. airport. Strobe Talbott, who described the latter incident in his book *Engaging India: Diplomacy, Democracy and the Bomb*, stated, "[He] (Fernandes) and other Indians who later referred to the incident clearly regarded it as more than merely a lapse of protocol or just another example of the post-9/11 excesses and indignities that air travelers had to endure for the sake of security. . . . The Indians saw it as a symptom of a deep-rooted widespread condescension—or worse—on the part of the West toward the East."[79]

Chinese nationalism too is powered by the concept of victimization. It has been suggested that "the essence of Chinese nationalism" has rested on two doctrines—one notion composed of China as the central kingdom, the pivotal point around which other states revolve, and the belief that China "destined by its superior culture to tutor others was being ravished by Western barbarians."[80] As a consequence of the invasions and exploitations of the nineteenth century, China struggled with a "consciousness of backwardness" and a "crisis of cultural identity." China found itself "victimized, forced to grant extra-territorial privileges, sign 'unequal treaties' and pay reparations." China's greatness as a unique civilization came into question. Chinese thinkers struggled over how to redefine China to enable it to face the world.[81]

"The memory of 'national humiliation' is a strong element of national rhetoric but it is more than that. . . . In contrast to the self-confident American nationalism of manifest destiny, Chinese nationalism is powered by feelings of national humiliation and pride."[82] As in India, this sentiment has endured even as the contours of nationalism have changed. Modern Chinese anti-imperialist nationalism arose under Sun Yatsen, as a response to the humiliations and exploitation of the Opium Wars and the Treaty of Shimonoseki. It continued with the Guomindang regime and survived the Communist revolution to persist under the CCP government led by Mao. Indeed in 1949, when the CCP came to power, Mao proudly declared, "[T]he Chinese people have stood up" (*zhongguoren zhanqilaile*). His statement was an assertion that China had fought off foreign oppression and would not again tolerate such humiliations.

Today, China still bears the scars of past humiliations suffered at the hands of outsiders. It is not only highly sensitive to past and present injuries, real and imagined, but it constantly seeks to remind the world of its victim status. For example, the 1999 U.S. bombing of the Chinese embassy in Belgrade sparked massive outrage in China. The United States was baffled at the virulence of the anti-U.S. sentiment and the Chinese refusal to accept the U.S. explanation that the embassy's targeting was a clear mistake. Confused U.S. policy-makers assumed that the Chinese leadership must have been the reason that Chinese public opinion had spun out of control, criticizing Beijing for its failure to inform Chinese citizens that the attack was a mistake.

Gries points out that the United States just could not understand the depth of Chinese anger arising out of "national narratives of China's early modern victimization at the hands of imperialism."[83] From China's perspective, the United States constantly sought to suppress Chinese aspirations and denigrate them. The bombing was simply another manifestation of this attitude. In 2001, the international furor over the collision of a U.S. Navy EP-3 reconnaissance aircraft and a Chinese F-8 fighter jet resulted from China's portrayal that the United States showed a reckless disregard for both Chinese sovereignty and Chinese lives.

The question, raised earlier in this chapter, of to what extent memories of humiliation are deliberately constructed is an interesting one. It is indisputable that colonizing states designed imperial and colonial institutions to dominate the subordinate society, structures that contained within them elements of racism and exploitation. As a consequence, many events and incidents of humiliation that the Chinese or Indians draw upon to construct their narratives were real. However, an understandable sensitivity to slights and insults may also generate narratives of abuse and harm amplified beyond what the historical record supports.

The Nanjing Massacre provides one such example. This real incident of

absolute horror and trauma led to Chinese hypersensitivity to any real or perceived harm by Japan, which has the result, claim the Japanese, of exaggerating
their wartime atrocities. Similarly, India refuses to acknowledge any possible
benefits of British colonial rule, even India's enduring and impressive railway
system. This system, it is indignantly pointed out, was created only to exploit
India all the more efficiently. In fact, the press and opposition wrathfully criticized a July 2005 speech by Indian prime minister Manmohan Singh at Oxford
University for touching upon the beneficial legacies of colonial rule.[84] These
excesses in criticism, however, do not negate the conviction shared by both
India and China, that they have been unjustly used and exploited, and are victims.

The dominant goal of victimhood drives the two subordinate goals of PII.
The memories of suffering and the sense of entitlement and recovery drive
these states to maximize territorial sovereignty and status. The goal of maximizing territorial sovereignty is synonymous with an insistence on maintaining the
traditional borders that were redrawn by colonialism and efforts to regain "lost"
territory, often at the expense of material security. This subordinate goal is a
direct result of colonialism in two ways.

First, the idea of unambiguous political boundaries is a product of colonialism. There is a sharp distinction between pre-colonial and post-colonial
borders. The result of imperialism and colonialism was to shatter pre-colonial
borders and redraw territorial lines. Colonial empires mimicked the centralized
structures and unitary ideologies of sovereignty prevalent in European nation-
states. The newly independent post-colonial states in turn inherited these often
arbitrary boundaries and concomitant "poisoned legacies."[85]

This often resulted in completely changed notions of sovereignty, especially
territorial sovereignty, from fluid to rigid. Both India and China are prominent
examples of this change in the concept of territorial sovereignty. Like other pre-
colonial states, India and China had very loose concepts of territorial boundaries that were often ill-defined rather than strict lineal demarcations of territory.
Frontiers between states were often fuzzily demarcated nebulous zones. When
borders were marked precisely, the markers such as boundary stones "became
points of reference only in specific instances of need or dispute."[86] "[C]arto-
graphic anxiety over territorial possessions was new to the area and was spread
via colonialism to distant parts of the globe."[87]

During the pre–Opium War period of the Qing, China's foreign relations
with the "barbarians" (unsinicized peoples) was organized through a tributary
system. The barbarians recognized Chinese suzerainty through regular tribute
missions to Peking, where they kowtowed before the Chinese emperor, whose

imperial writ encompassed all civilization. In return for this recognition, the emperor bestowed lavish gifts upon them. Under this system, China had no fixed boundaries. "This web was organized in a concentric arc of frontier territory surrounding China proper, with the nearer boundary of the territory forming an inner frontier with China and the outer extremity of the tributary state forming an outer frontier with the lands beyond. This band of territory changed in size according to the fortunes of the tributary peoples and their changing relations, both with China and with the alien peoples in the other direction."[88] The Chinese name for China (*zhongguo*) sums up this relationship—it translates as "Middle Kingdom," implying that China was the center of all civilization surrounded by subordinate territories. Despite disagreement about the exact nature of China's traditional relationship with its neighboring states, as an empire the idea of sovereignty did not feature in its outlook—"the question of delineation of interstate borders simply did not exist."[89]

In India, both the period of the Mughal empire and the period between the decline of the Mughals and the ascent of the British were characterized by political decentralization. Even during the height of its power under Emperor Akbar, when the Mughals had territorial control over much of the subcontinent, conquered territories were ruled either by the original king who now swore allegiance to the Mughals or through a descendant of the existing ruling family, who was set up as head of state by the emperor. Thus a network of alliances was built up with the regional rulers who were drawn into defending and administering the empire through the *mansabdari* system. *Mansab* means "rank," and a *mansabdar* was the holder of an official rank of anything from ten to five thousand and sometimes even ten thousand. A *mansabdar* of ten was expected to have ten men under his command and so on. Other than these tasks, these regional rulers remained largely autonomous.[90] According to Bayly,

> [T]he Mughals claimed universal dominion; sometimes they achieved political dominance in India. But for the majority of their Hindu subjects power and authority in India had always been more like a complicated hierarchy than a scheme of "administration" or "government." The Mughal emperor was *Shah-an-Shah*, "king of kings," rather than king of India. He was the highest manifestation of sovereignty, the court of final appeal, for Muslims an earthly successor to aspects of the authority of the Prophet Mohammad. Yet many of the attributes of what we would call the state pertained not to the emperor or his lieutenants, but to the Hindu kings of the localities, the rajas or to the notables who controlled resources and authority in the villages. The emperor's power and wealth could be great, but only if he was skilled in extracting money, soldiers and devotion from other kings. He was a marshal of kings, an entrepreneur in power . . . some historians have described this political system in terms of "levels of power."[91]

Second, territorial sovereignty is so central to PII because new states emerged in situations in which differences in pre- and post-colonial borders led to civil wars, formerly held territories being lost, and partitions of formerly intact political units. Consequently, India and China harbor bitter resentment for the territorial damage inflicted on them by imperialist states and are determined not to give way on traditional territorial boundaries that are intimately tied to their nationalist beliefs and, hence, their identity.

Acharya calls Asia "the most sovereignty-bound region in the world,"[92] while Johnston writes, "China is clearly 'constrained' by a particularly extensive and absolutist version of the sovereignty norm. It may be argued that China's version of sovereignty comes closer than most to the Westphalian ideal. Much of Chinese foreign policy practice, particularly after 1989, has focused on the vigorous defense of China's own sovereignty and the sovereignty of others. Indeed as an explanatory variable, the strength of Chinese adherence to the sovereignty norm provides more insights into Chinese foreign policy than any tendency to power balance in the neorealist sense."[93]

The idea of territorial sovereignty, thus, arrived late in both China and India when the advent of Western powers in China and the British in India resulted in stricter definitions of boundaries. When it did arrive, however, the consequent rigid stance on traditional borders and "lost" territories was driven by the consciousness that traditional borders had been invaded and plundered by colonial powers and territories had been lost because of colonial machinations. For China, the territories lost by the Qing as a result of "unequal" treaties resulted in an obsession with "rightfully" reclaiming pieces of territory and a rejection of colonial boundaries. Carlson states that "as is well known to even the casual observer of Chinese politics, China has gone to great lengths during the 1990s to defend both its territorial claims to contested border regions and its jurisdictional claims over Taiwan and Tibet."[94]

India's position was more complex. As the former Indian diplomat J. N. Dixit acknowledged, the Indians are "selective" on the issue of accepting colonial territorial arrangements.[95] They completely adopted the boundaries drawn by the colonial British administration because they believed that these simply formalized the boundaries of the territories that had been controlled by previous Indian dynasties, including the Mughals and the Sikhs. But they were traumatized by the loss of territory that the creation of Pakistan entailed. They blamed this on British policies of divide-and-rule without which, they believed, Jinnah's ideology could not have succeeded. Given that the national goal of maximizing territorial sovereignty is driven by memories of victimization and loss, the issue of secession of particular territories is particularly sensitive and dealt with harshly. Indian and Chinese attitudes toward Kashmir, Punjab, Taiwan, Tibet and Xinjiang have always been tied to the anti-imperial, anti-colonial national identity.

Besides the desire to preserve and protect territorial boundaries and regain lost territories, PII encompasses another goal: the advancement of status. Research has shown that the "prestige motive" whereby political groups pursue prestige as an end in itself can be an important factor influencing the behavior of states.[96] Status is particularly important to India and China, since the humiliations of imperialism and colonialism created a desire to regain prestige in the international system and recover lost esteem. Nehru, for example, strongly believed that "Asian countries needed to find a way of relating as equals to the richer powers of the Western world."[97]

In India, the rise of nationalism after the Revolt of 1857 and the takeover of the Crown centered on the efforts of the intelligentsia to restore the pride in the Indian people. While there was a dispute between reformers who sought to incorporate Western rationalist thought into Indian traditions to achieve this end and revivalists who pursued the renewal of age-old customs and beliefs, both programs of action sought to recapture past glory and instill a sense of pride in Indian culture. The effort was to fashion an "anti-colonial modernity."[98] Partha Chatterjee has argued that these two arguments often coexisted in nationalist thinking. Chatterjee observes that anti-colonial nationalism in Asia and Africa can be divided into material and spiritual domains. The former—containing science, technology, the economy and statecraft—were areas of clear Western dominance in which Eastern replication and emulation were necessary to compete. The latter referred to a distinctness of cultural identity. Chatterjee argued they were reconciled through a belief that "the greater one's success in imitating Western skills in the material domain, the greater the need to preserve the distinctness of one's spiritual culture."[99]

Rising Chinese nationalism too laid special emphasis on the "consciousness of suffering" from disorder and humiliation in the hands of foreign powers and recapturing the past glory of Chinese history.[100] This is expressed through numerous phrases such as "the humiliation caused by foreign powers" (wai wu), "to wipe out the national shame and recover the fatherland" (xuechi fuguo), "the loss of economic rights to foreigners" (liquan waiyi) and to "guard against the insults of foreign powers (yu wu).[101]

William Callahan who has written extensively about Chinese national humiliation points out that the "discursive twin" of national humiliation is "national salvation." Taking care to avoid the loss of face and regaining lost status is an important component of that salvation.[102] Both Nehru's and Mao's writings, among those of other nationalists, clearly reflect the pride taken in Indian and Chinese culture and ancient status, and the blame assigned to the colonialists for the destruction of that privileged position and the humiliation they heaped on the formerly ascendant country.

The sensitivity to issues of status has resulted in behavior that neorealists, with their belief in security-maximizing states, would find unusual. In 1996, China signed the Comprehensive Test Ban Treaty even though a number of its military and nuclear weapons specialists were opposed, arguing that it would give China a permanent position of inferiority in warhead design options. As it turned out, Beijing was far more concerned that it would be identified as the "isolated spoiler of a treaty that had long been considered a pillar of the non-proliferation regime."[103]

What exactly is considered "prestigious" by these states can of course change depending on who the victimizer is perceived to be. An excellent example is the issue of India and permanent membership in the UN Security Council. In the 1950s Nehru was offered a permanent seat by the United States,[104] but he spurned the offer, citing solidarity with the People's Republic of China whose UN seat was occupied by the Republic of China (Taiwan). In this instance the victimizer was perceived to be the United States, with its bullying ways, and it was prestigious for India to take the high moral road by refusing the dominating Western powers. In the twenty-first century, the situation has changed. India, a confident nuclear power, expects a permanent seat in the Security Council as a prestigious prerequisite befitting its position as a rising power. The victimizer today is the "club of nuclear powers" hell bent on denying India its rightful status.

Many states try to maximize territorial sovereignty and status, but India and China, as PII states, have a sense of entitlement and recovery that is the corollary of the goal of victimhood and drives the subordinate goals of territorial sovereignty and status. Given their experience of colonial trauma and the loss of territory and prestige, they seek to either recover or guard against "lost" territories, and regain face. This amplified pursuit of these goals, even when security or economic well-being are threatened, characterizes PII states.

Conclusion

PII, a product of colonial trauma, matters in three very important ways. First, it offers a new way to analyze and understand the behavior of two crucial states, India and China. Because of India's and China's status as rising powers, most analyses focus on state security and growing capabilities as the dominant explanatory variables of their behavior. The evidence presented above demonstrates the resonance and emphasis placed in national discourse on the colonial past. This instills a sense of victimhood and, its corollary, a sense of entitlement to recover and receive restitution for past losses. Understanding the source of these demands, generated for reasons distinct from state security and national capabilities, should be an important component of any international discourse on "managing" or "engaging" these two rising powers. Callahan has pointed out the influence of themes of past humiliation and victimization in twenty-first-century Chinese nationalism,[105] highlighting that "the theme of the 2004 National Defense Education Fund, for example, was 'never forget national humiliation, strengthen our national defense.'"[106] Any analysis of China's fraught relationship with Japan, which led to large anti-Japanese violence and riots in 2005, needs to incorporate the Chinese preoccupation with past victimization at the hands of Japan. India's justification for its nuclear tests in 1998 included references to ending the era of "nuclear apartheid" that delineated "nuclear haves and have-nots," while also invoking the classic colonial imagery of breaking into the "club of nuclear powers."[107] Understanding India's pursuit of nuclear power status with references only to security or even prestige is, therefore, incomplete without an understanding of its grievance against a nuclear system that it believed was specifically designed to exclude and discriminate.

Second, PII is important to the study of international politics because it systematically treats history, specifically colonialism, as a causal variable. By examining trauma theory and colonialism as collective historical trauma, it shows how the narrative of suffering and victimhood became a component of the national identity of India and China. Many theories of international behavior are ahistorical. Even when some states are labeled revisionist or status quo, the origins of those preferences are left unspecified. PII explains how historical experiences can generate state goals.

Third, PII is generalizable. In emphasizing the transformative historical event of colonialism, thereby underlining the simple but overlooked fact that history matters, it ensures that the international behavior of a wide range of states with differing regimes and power structures can be analyzed. Theories of offensive and defensive realism and predictions of state behavior such as balancing, bandwagoning or bargaining refer primarily to states with material capabilities significant enough to matter, while norm-based theories focus on states with the ability to impose or break norms.[108] The behavior of developing nations tends to be given short shrift, and when they do receive attention, the assumption is that disparities in economic structures and material capabilities are the sole criteria for distinguishing them from developed nations.[109]

A large category of states—states that have experienced imperialism and colonialism—do not necessarily behave in the way that realists or liberals would necessarily predict because a common transformative historical event contributes to a powerful ideology of victimhood that dominates their decision calculus. Thus the transformative historical event of colonialism can be an important tool to categorize states and explain variations in state foreign policies. This categorization, and associated traits that follow from it, may be better able to explain key features of foreign policy than traditional dichotomies such as developed versus developing states, major versus minor powers, and revisionist versus status quo states.

While it is beyond the scope of this book to examine each and every state in the world that has experienced extractive colonialism and measure the impact of that episode on foreign policy after decolonization, it can be shown that the discourse of victimhood is evident in these countries even today. The following chapter analyzes speeches of states in the United Nations to show that there is a statistically significant difference between the discourse of states that have been colonized and those that have not. That difference is attributable to a sense of victimhood.

PII: Discord and Discourse in the UN

Introduction

More than a half-century after decolonization, it might be surprising if PII with its emphasis on victimhood was still evident in the discourse of states that had experienced colonialism, particularly if we think of all the global changes in the years since these states became independent. In the intervening decades, new leaders and states have emerged, wars have been fought, dominant economic beliefs have come and gone, communications have been revolutionized, to name just a few major changes. As this chapter shows, these changes have not eliminated the goal of victimhood that sits at the center of PII. The desire to be recognized and empathized with as a victim in the international system has endured among these states, something that can be demonstrated by showing that there is a statistically significant difference in the discourse of states that have been colonized and states that have not.

This chapter lays out a test to demonstrate the existence of PII, and proceeds to uncover the differences between states that experienced extractive colonialism and those that did not. It does so by using a new method that I developed to statistically analyze the content of 2,545 UN General Debate speeches from 1993 to 2007.

In order to show the existence of PII, my approach is two-tiered. First, using a new method of content analysis, I establish that there are statistically significant differences between the public discourse of colonized states and non-colonized states. This method determines the distributions of all words used by colonial and non-colonial states, and those distributions are then compared with distributions from alternative categorizations. By comparing these distributions—in effect, reducing the usage of hundreds of millions of words into easily identifiable usage differences—it is possible to identify, with known statistical significance, real differences in discourse based on the colonial status of states.

Second, I then extensively study the usage of the words within the context of the speeches and demonstrate that this statistically significant difference between colonized and non-colonized states can be largely attributed to words that exhibit a strong sense of victimization. Specifically, as outlined in the previous chapter, PII has three components: maximizing the goals of victimhood, territorial sovereignty, and status. The goal of maximizing victimhood is the central component of PII and underlines the adherence to the goals of maximizing territorial sovereignty and status. Thus, the most striking and important outcome of my analysis is that a significant portion of the differences between colony and non-colony speeches can be attributed to words that exhibit a strong sense of victimization. As I will show, the goals of maximizing sovereignty and status are often implicit within the context of victimization.

Discourse in the United Nations: The General Debate

Public discourse is a reflection of states' beliefs and a predictor of their impending behavior. Thus a method of categorizing different patterns of state beliefs and anticipating behavior is by analyzing their speeches and statements in international forums. The public discourse chosen for analysis here is well over a decade of UN General Debate speeches from 1993 to 2007.

While voting behavior is also a method of analyzing state positions on issues, there is a possibility of bias in the issues chosen for analysis. In analyzing political discourse, I am not choosing particular speeches or offering a dictionary of words that *should* be present.[1] Rather I am going to analyze *every* word in *every* speech made by *every* country in *every* year in the time period under observation. Rather than analyzing a list of words picked by me, I am analyzing the discourse of every member of the United Nations to show that there is a statistical difference between the discourse of countries that have experienced extractive colonialism and those that have not. The speeches of the United Nations were chosen because it is the largest international organization in the world.

One week after the opening of the annual session of the General Assembly and the adoption of its agenda, the member states take part in a General Debate.

The Debate has a long history, dating back to the second session and all subsequent regular sessions of the Assembly. It is an important diplomatic event with the majority of the 192 member states participating every year. It usually lasts for an uninterrupted period of nine working days, and the speeches are made by high-level dignitaries including heads of state, heads of government and foreign ministers. While there is no formal provision in the Rules of Procedure for a General Debate, the 1963 committee on procedure outlined it as "a series of statements made by most Chairmen of delegations on world problems and the role of the United Nations, in the light of the annual report of the Secretary-General on the work of the Organization and reports of other United Nations organs."[2] The Debate ends when all members who wish to participate have made their speeches.

The 1993–2007 General Debate speeches were selected for a number of reasons. First, selection of these speeches ensured the universe of cases includes all member states of the United Nations. Since no other international body has a larger number of members, this maximized the representation and variety of states being examined. Second, as Bailey points out, "[T]he Debate itself has certain intrinsic values—it is a barometer which indicates changes in the international climate and it has also been compared to a safety valve because it enables governments to let off steam on contentious issues without causing undue damage."[3] Members can therefore candidly express their opinions on all international issues including those which may not be formally discussed by the Assembly. For example, in the 1960s, when the Assembly decided not to discuss the issue of Chinese representation in the United Nations, the General Debate provided an outlet for the members to state their views. The Debate speeches therefore ensure that the discourse being analyzed often represents the forthright opinions of states.

Third, the Assembly, unlike, say, the Security Council, ensures an equal forum for discussion and debate to all member states. Every member state, irrespective of size, has one seat and one vote. Fourth, the time span 1993–2007 was selected as the least likely period to show evidence of victimhood. The bulk of decolonization took place in the 1950s and 1960s, and it is to be expected that any memories of humiliation and victimhood would be present immediately following decolonization rather than in the contemporary era.

According to the logic of PII, one would expect that the speeches of states that have experienced colonialism would, first, have a perception of the self as a victim; second, indicate a need to be recognized by the international community as such, often in conjunction with condemning the actions of an "other";

and third, often express sympathy and solidarity with other states that are per-ceived to have been "victimized" in a similar fashion. It is important to recognize here that perception of the self as a victim and the need to be recognized as such does not necessarily imply a direct reference to the impact of colonialism. Direct references to colonial history and exploitation, while important, are only a part of the general goal of being recognized as a victim in the international system. Once conditioned by the trauma inflicted under colonialism to think of their role as victim, these states are likely to see their own victimization in novel circumstances.

Methodology[4]

The UN has 192 member states.[5] The first step was to create a dataset of states and their colonial status. Drawing from the ICOW Colonial History dataset,[6] the states were divided into two categories—Category 1 (C_1) includes all states that have experienced some form of extractive colonialism in the past four hundred years; Category 2 (C_2) includes non-colonized states.[7]

Definitions

Claim: If PII exists there should be a difference in the discourse between the states in category C_1 and category C_2.

I first statistically analyze the usage of words by C_1 and C_2 states to determine whether there are any statistically significant differences in their word usage.[8] This is an obvious and necessary first step: if there are no differences in the word usage, there is no point continuing the analysis.

To conduct the analysis, I first make a Total Word List (TWL) of all the words used in all the speeches from 1993 to 2007.[9] Words that are used in exactly one or exactly two speeches are discarded from the TWL. This primarily eliminates misspelled words, numbers, odd abbreviations, and acronyms, and of course a few rarely used vocabulary words, all of which are not helpful in the analysis. I have checked that this does not alter the outcome of the analysis, but it does significantly reduce noise and hard-to-handle "long-tail" distribution artifacts in the results. What remains are 19,392 words used in at least three different speeches. I then count the total number of times each remaining word $i = 1$, 2, ... , 19,392 in the TWL is used by C_1 states and by C_2 states yielding counts $W_i^{C_1}$ and $W_i^{C_2}$. The total word count for each category is the sum of these word counts,

$$T^{C_1} = \Sigma_{i=1}^{19392} W_i^{C_1} = 4.41 \times 10^6 \text{ and } T^{C_2} = \Sigma_{i=1}^{19392} W_i^{C_2} = 1.38 \times 10^6.$$

Next, for each word I determine two fractions:

$$f_i^{C_1} = \frac{W_i^{C_1}}{T_i^{C_1}} \text{ and } f_i^{C_2} = \frac{W_i^{C_2}}{T_i^{C_2}}.$$

The fraction $f_i^{C_1}$ is the fraction of times that C_1 states use word i out of all other words. Of course $f_i^{C_2}$ is the fraction of times that C_2 states use word i, where $W_i^{C_1}$ is the total number of times a word is used by C_1 states and $W_i^{C_2}$ is the total number of times a word is used by C_2 states. There are more C_1 states than C_2 states, and not all speeches contain the same number of words. However, by studying the fraction of times a word is used (instead of total counts or some other statistic), we are in a sense studying the probability of words being used, which effectively normalizes the speech-to-speech and category-to-category differences.

With these definitions, I can now determine whether any given word is used an equal number of times by C_1 and C_2 states or whether it is used significantly more by C_1 states. To visually check this, I plot all words i with the $f_i^{C_1}$ value on the y-axis versus the $f_i^{C_2}$ value on the x-axis. If $f_i^{C_1} = f_i^{C_2}$ (that is, C_1 and C_2 states use word i with equal frequency) then these words will fall on the line of equality (LoE). As an important control on the methodology, I verified that very commonly used words, such as "the" and "and," appear most frequently in the content and, importantly, fall on the LoE (see Fig. 2.1). The further from the LoE, the greater the observed difference in the use of that word by C_1 and C_2 states. Since the fractions vary over several orders of magnitude, this is easier to see on a log plot (see Fig. 2.2). To quantify this difference in usage of any word i by the two categories, we define a difference parameter D_i:

$$D_i = \log(f_i^{C_1}) - \log(f_i^{C_2}).$$

This is an intuitive definition of D_i, as can be seen by looking at the log plot of $f_i^{C_1}$ vs. $f_i^{C_2}$ (see Fig. 2.3).

In fact, in comparison with several other plausible definitions of D_i (all of which yield similar results in the end), this definition is found to be most convenient.

To get a better intuitive feel for the D_i, note that when $D_i = 1$ then the C_1 states use that word 10 times more frequently than C_2 states. Table 2.1 shows conversions for other values of D_i.[10]

Another important fact about the D_i is that if either C_1 or C_2 uses a particular word 0 times, that is,

$$f_i^{C_1} = 0 \text{ or } f_i^{C_2} = 0, \text{ then the } D_i \text{ is undefined.}$$

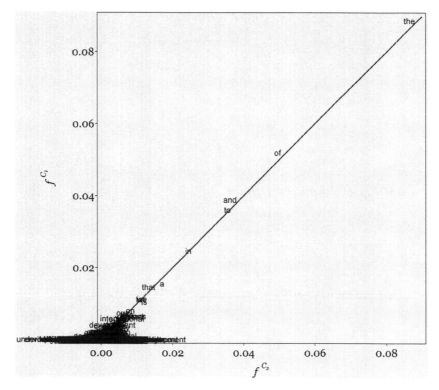

FIG. 2.1. All words plotted by their fractional use, including the line of equality. Source: Equation and figure created by author. Each word i in the TWL plotted with $f_i^{C_1}$ on the vertical axis and $f_i^{C_2}$ on the horizontal axis. The *LoE* is shown. Notice on the linear scale that most words fall below $f = 0.001$, indicating that a log graph may be more useful (see Fig. 2.2). Words such as "the," "of," "and," "to," etc. are used most frequently and fall very near the *LoE*, which is to be expected.

Statistical Analysis

I now move on to analyze the distribution of difference parameters to determine whether the use of words by C_1 states and C_2 states is significantly different. Since I am analyzing a large number of words, I will have some distribution of D_i values. This distribution contains information about the difference in language use between the colonized and non-colonized countries. Obviously, there will be variations in the usage of words resulting from natural differences in the topics of speeches and the usage of language. My goal is to show that there is more variation between C_1 and C_2 states than there would be between randomly chosen groups of states.

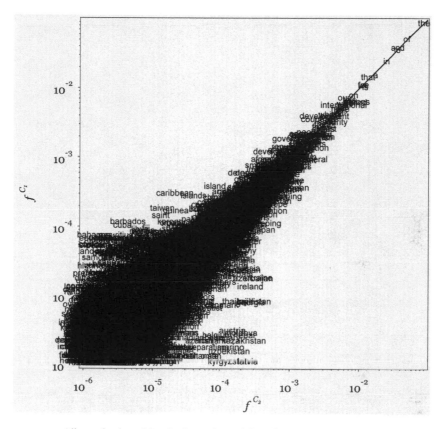

FIG. 2.2. All words plotted by the logarithm of their fractional use, including the line of equality. Source: Created by author.

The first step is to find a way to represent this distribution of D_i values. There are various ways to represent this distribution D_i. One way is to create histograms to count the number of words that are used more often by each category.[11] Quantiles of the D_i values can be obtained by sorting the D_i values, and plotting them against the word number i.

This effectively creates a discrete cumulative distribution function (CDF), as shown in Fig. 2.4. Since the number of words is so large, this discrete CDF can be approximated by a continuous CDF by simple interpolation, as shown by the dashed curve. This has been shown to eliminate unwanted discretization noise in the data without changing the outcome. Finally, this CDF can be differentiated to generate an estimate of the normalized probability density function (PDF) of this set of D_i values, as shown in Figs. 2.5 and 2.6. Now, I can measure

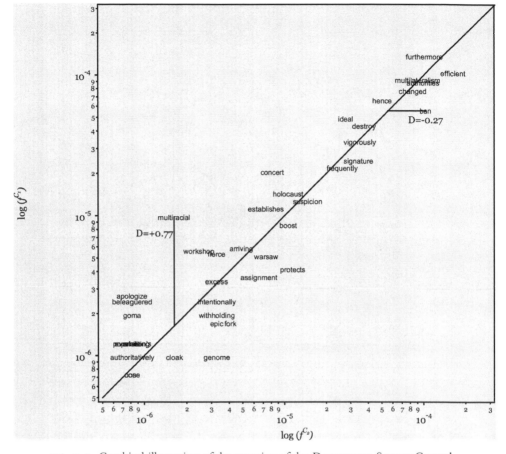

FIG. 2.3. Graphical illustration of the meaning of the *D* parameter. Source: Created by author. This is the same as Fig. 2.2 except showing only 50 randomly selected words for clarity. Two example *D* values are shown graphically to reinforce the intuitive graphical definition of *D* as a distance from the *LoE*. Notice that even though the word "multiracial" is used almost 10 times less than "ban" by all countries, the relevant fact that it is used about 6 times more by C_1 states than C_2 states is captured by its higher *D* value.

the natural, random variation in word usage by choosing random categories. I can then show that the difference between C_1 and C_2 categories is greater than this natural variation.

To demonstrate that there is an increase in the differences between C_1 and C_2 due to PII, I perform a randomized test. I first create 200 alternative category pairs: $C_1^{*1}, C_1^{*2}, ..., C_1^{*200}$ and $C_2^{*1}, C_2^{*2}, ..., C_2^{*200}$.

Each alternative category pair (C_1^{*i} and C_2^{*i}) is composed of a random parti-

TABLE 2.1. D Conversion Values

D_i	×More
0.25	1.8
0.5	3.2
0.75	5.6
1	10
1.25	17.8
2	100

Source. All tables were created by the author.

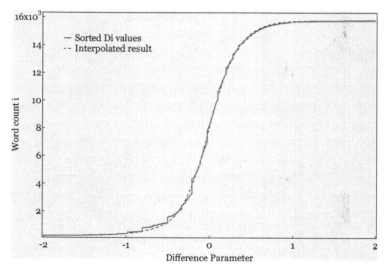

FIG. 2.4. Quantile plot of the D parameter. Source: Created by author. D_i values for each are sorted from smallest to largest, and plotted along the bottom axis against their sorted order. This common statistical technique generates a "quantile" plot, as shown. Interpolation yields the dashed curve, which smooths the jumps that result from the fact that the data (i.e., word counts) are in fact discrete, not continuous.

tioning of the 192 countries. Note that the number of countries in each C_1^{*i} is equal to the number of countries in C_1 (and the same for C_2).[12] In other words, I create 200 alternative ways to randomly partition the 192 countries other than simply by colonial status.

Using the alternative C^* partitions, I calculate 200 sets of f^{*C_1} and f^{*C_2} values, from which I calculate 200 alternative sets of D^* parameters. I construct 200 normalized probability density functions (PDFs) of these D^* parameters to determine the distribution of the natural variation in word usage.

Next, I create an average PDF from these 200 PDFs, and calculate the stan-

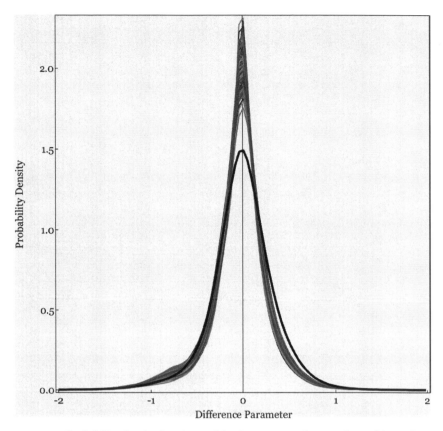

FIG. 2.5. Probability density functions of the D parameter. Source: Created by author. Estimated probability density functions of the D values of the 200 random partitions are shown in assorted grey thin lines, and the estimated density function of the D values of the categorization by colony is shown in bold black. Notice that there is a region between about $D \sim 0.16$ and $D \sim 1.2$ where the colonial status density is higher than any of the random PDFs; this indicates that there is a difference in the word usage between C_1 and C_2 states that cannot be explained just by natural variation.

dard deviation δ of each bin. I checked (via quantile-quantile plots) that the variations between the random speeches can be represented by normally distributed random noise, so the standard deviation can be treated as the standard deviation of normally distributed noise (as would be expected from a large data set). Thus, 3δ (3 standard deviation) error bars represent a 99.6 percent confidence interval. In other words, there is only a 0.4 percent chance that the number of counts would fall outside the confidence interval merely by chance.

Finally, I compare the PDF of D_i values from the categorization based on colonial status to this "standard" PDF. As can be seen in Figure 2.7 there are

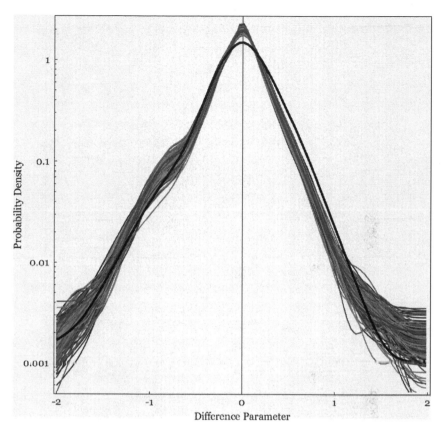

FIG. 2.6. Logarithm of the probability density functions of the D parameter. Source: Created by author. The same as Fig. 2.5 but on a log scale to better indicate the behavior in the tails of the distribution.

several regions of D where the word-count falls well outside the confidence interval of the standard distribution. The D_i range between 0.16 and 1.2 has significantly higher probability density for words in the D distribution than would have been expected randomly based on the D^* distribution.

So, for example, if we count the number of words with $D_i \sim 0.3$ (representing words that are used twice as often by C_1 states as C_2 states), we see that there are typically about 1000 words that C_1^* states use twice as many times as C_2^* states. But we see that when states are categorized by colonial status there are about 40 percent more extra words that are used by twice as many times by C_1 states than by C_2 states than would have been expected just as a result of typical (random) differences of word usage. This is similarly true for words used in the other significant regions. The elevated counts of words in these regions strongly suggest there are a significant number of words that are used more by states that

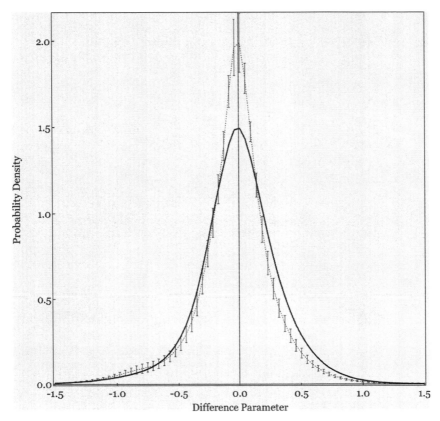

FIG. 2.7. Logarithm of the averaged probability density functions showing significant differences in word usage. Source: Created by author. The dashed grey line indicates the average word count from the 200 random distributions (see Fig. 2.5). The error bars show the 99.6 percent confidence interval ($\pm 3\sigma$) calculated from these same random probability density functions. The black curve is the distribution of D values (the important partition based on colonial status). Note the region between $D \sim 0.16$ and $D \sim 1.2$ where the black curve is significantly higher than the dashed grey curve, indicating a significant difference in word usage between C_1 and C_2 states that cannot be explained by natural variations of word usage (which are captured in the D^* probability density function). We will later examine whether these differences in word usage can be attributed to PII.

have been colonized than those that have not.[13] This alone, of course, does not show that PII exists. In order to determine if these differences are due to PII, I will have to analyze the words in context and check their usage.

Analysis

Words that fall into the statistically significant regions were sorted into four types. Type 0 (T_0) words are those that have no meaning or effect in

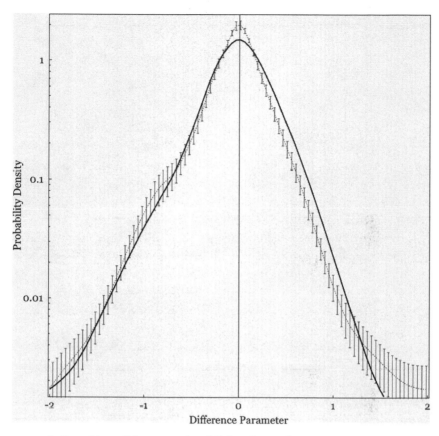

FIG. 2.8. Logarithm of the averaged probability density functions showing significant differences in word usage. The same as Fig. 2.7 but with log vertical axis to better illustrate the difference.

terms of PII or are simply typographic errors in the speech. For example, words like *receives*, *substances*, *publication* or *wake* fall into this category. Type 1 (T_1) words are those that clearly indicate the existence of PII. Type 2 (T_2) words are proper nouns—country names, people names and so forth. Since states tend to refer to themselves and their leaders continuously through the speech, these words fall into the statistically significant regions. Type 3 (T_3) words are those that may be indicative of PII depending on how each country uses them. The largest number of words fall under T_3 since it is difficult to declare categorically that a word is indicative of PII without reading through each speech and checking how it is used in each case. For example, words like *scourge* or *intrusive* would fall into this category. However the presence of these words certainly does not negate the evidence in favor of PII and often bolsters it.

To establish that T_1 words as used in the speeches show the presence of PII, I generated a randomly selected list of eight C_1 states for each of the fifteen years. I then checked through the T_1 words used by them in each speech to see how they were used. The lowest D among the T_1 words is 0.16, which means that even the least amount of times C_1 states use that word is still almost 1.5 times more than C_2 states. Each country used the words to convey a sense of victimhood. By a sense of victimhood I mean that these states felt themselves to have been victimized, and this was conveyed not just through an expression of the self as victim but also by an obvious desire for the international community to recognize them as victims, by condemnation of an "other," or by an expression of solidarity with a state perceived to have also been victimized. The sense of victimhood also sometimes reflects the fact that many C_1 states are developing states. However the difference between C_1 and C_2 is not simply one of rich and poor or powerful and non-powerful states. Ireland and Israel, for example, are C_1 states whereas Ethiopia and Uzbekistan are C_2 states. In fact nearly 50 percent of C_2 states are low- and middle-income states. Moreover, the C_1 states' complaints about their developing status or their lack of influence is often directly linked by them to the history of colonialism.

I start with words that refer to the historical context of PII. As is to be expected, C_1 states refer much more to colonial history and its effects than C_2 states. They also refer repeatedly to the Non-Aligned Movement (NAM), which was essentially composed of states that had undergone decolonization as well as shared similar histories of oppression. Table 2.2 gives examples of words used to refer to historical experiences and how many times more C_1 states use these words than C_2 states.

We can see from Table 2.2, C_1 states refer to *colonialism* 3.7 times more and *colonized* 6.8 times more than C_2 states. This is particularly interesting given that the bulk of decolonization took place in the 1950s and 1960s, and for some even earlier than that. In 1993, for example, President Fujimori of Peru stated, "In 1990, the Peruvian people heirs to an ancient culture, who, like other peoples of the Third World, suffered the consequences of colonialism and later various frustrations caused by our history, began to ask themselves more and more why they had not reached a truly dignified level of existence comparable to that of the developed countries." In this particular case, in addition to the portrayal of Peru as victim, there is also an identification with other victimized states and an implicit linking of colonialism to current backwardness.

Similarly, India echoed these sentiments in 1995: "Most Members of the United Nations joined immediately after emerging from colonial rule, with their economies destroyed, and dependent on foreign languages for communication,

TABLE 2.2. Selected Words and D Values I

Word	D_i	×More
Legacies	0.2	1.5
Colonialists	0.32	2.1
Subjugated	0.38	2.4
Colonial	0.44	2.8
Colonialism	0.57	3.7
Colonization	0.62	4.2
Non-aligned	0.7	5
Colonized	0.83	6.8
Subjugation	0.87	7.4

on imperial capitals for support and on donors for subsistence." Burundi, in 2001, even suggested the prevalence of colonialism in the twenty-first century: "Yet another issue of concern to my delegation continues to be that of human dignity, which cannot be conceived as divorced from respect for human rights, including that of self-determination. Towards that end, the delegation of Burundi continues to hope that the Second International Decade for the Elimination of Colonialism, from 2001 to 2010, proclaimed by the Assembly by its resolution 55/146 of 8 December 2000, will help to eradicate its last bastions."

Despite the almost complete irrelevance of NAM in the post-1990s, after the blocs to which states could align had disappeared, C_1 states still seem to give weight to the proclamations and opinions of the NAM community and refer to it often. Table 2.2 shows that C_1 states refer to it five times as much as C_2 states. In 1993, Syria congratulated President Insanally of the General Assembly and "commended" him on the "role of his friendly country in the Non-Aligned Movement." In 1998, Sudan cited the Non-Aligned Movement as one of its supporters against American cruise missile strikes that had occurred that year. As recently as 2004, Cuba declared, "We, as non-aligned countries, will have to entrench ourselves in defending the United Nations Charter, because if we do not it will be redrafted with the deletion of every trace of such principles as the sovereign equality of States, non-intervention and the non-use or the threat of use of force. . . . Let us revitalize the Non-Aligned Movement."

In keeping with this sensitivity to the history of oppression and dominance, subjugation is used 7.4 times more by C_1 states (see Table 2.2). In 1998, the Democratic Republic of Congo declared, "The Assembly will agree with me that no honourable nation can allow its sovereignty and territorial integrity to be called into question. The Congolese people will never accept subjugation, oppression or the imposition of perverse values." In 1999, Armenia referred to the ethnic conflict in Azerbaijan and stated, "First and foremost, Armenia must ensure that the Armenian population of Nagorny Karabakh continues to enjoy its security within its own lands. Our recent memories of vulnerability and insecurity make it impossible for any Armenian anywhere to accept anything less than the inalienable right of the people of Nagorny Karabakh not to be subjugated, not to be dominated, and not to be subordinate." Armenia's statement demonstrates how the colonial past of C_1 states make them highly sensitive to other similar histories or incidents of domination. To take still another example, in 1993 Afghanistan condemned Soviet oppression and blamed it for their developmental problems: "One of the most damaging legacies that Afghanistan has inherited from Soviet occupation, Communist rule and the long, drawn-out war is a substantial break-up of our civil and military administration and the virtual collapse of our economic and financial institutions."

Three of the strongest indicators of victimhood and PII, follow from this sensitivity to past and present oppression. First, C_1 states are obsessed with the lack of parity between states in the international system. They object not just to the gaps between developed and developing states but also to power disparities between small and big states and in the international system in general. The sensitivity to the disparities in the international system implies that C_1 states are also sensitive to their perceived status in the international system. Table 2.3 lists some of the words that are used to express disparity, the D_i for that word, and how many times more C_1 states use the word compared with C_2 states.

In 1993, Algeria complained, "Whole regions, and even entire continents, are being marginalized in a most atrocious manner. The right of peoples to self-determination is being violated and obstructed here and there. Hunger and poverty are expanding. Imbalances in the world economy are deepening and worsening. All of these situations pose challenges to the international community that call for urgent and concerted action." In 1994, Ireland agreed, "We must intensify our efforts to eliminate the root causes of many conflicts—inequality, social injustice, and poverty—by acting on the Secretary-General's agenda for development. . . . Maintaining peace is impossible in an unequal world. Conversely, development is the most secure basis for peace."

In 1996, China pointed out, "Only by enhancing international exchanges and cooperation on the basis of equality and mutual benefit can we jointly cope with new problems arising in the course of world economic advances and achieve sustained common development and prosperity. No one should overlook the unevenness of world development and the ever widening gap between developed and developing countries. Caught in the web of relentless international competition, the least-developed countries are in distress, and the risk

TABLE 2.3. Selected Words and D Values II

Word	D_i	×More
Inequalities	0.18	1.5
Inequality	0.18	1.5
Equitable	0.19	1.5
Vulnerable	0.2	1.6
Disparities	0.21	1.6
Suffer	0.25	1.8
Equality	0.26	1.8
Disparity	0.3	2
Inequitable	0.3	2
Struggles	0.3	2
Inequity	0.38	2.4
Inequities	0.4	2.5
Unequal	0.41	2.6
Imbalance	0.47	3
Marginalized	0.51	3.2
Equitably	0.58	3.8
Asymmetries	0.59	3.9

of marginalization is looming large." In 1999, South Korea stated: "One consequence of globalization has been the widening gap between the developed and the developing countries and the increasing marginalization of the least developed ones. Unattended, the disparity will only grow in the twenty-first century of unlimited competition, becoming a risk factor that could endanger global stability and peace. There is a pressing need for a new paradigm of international development cooperation, whereby the chronic poverty and excessive debts besetting the developing countries and other related issues are taken as challenges to be overcome with the active input of all members of the global community." In 2002, Ghana, after referring to the "exploitative and unconscionable [effects of] colonialism," continued this oft-repeated theme of C_1 states: "We wish to recommend, however, that an organization such as the United Nations should provide the regulatory framework to ensure that the benefits of globalization are more equitably distributed."

In addition to the lack of parity between developed and developing nations, states complain about power imbalances. Madagascar's speech in 2003, for example, shows how significant it considers the power gap between big and small states: "We hope to see changes in our Organization that would place greater emphasis on the importance of the General Assembly as the principal deliberative and decision-making organ and on rendering the Security Council more representative and more transparent. Such reforms are necessary in order

TABLE 2.4. Selected Words and D Values III

Word	D_i	×More
Interference	0.18	1.5
Pressures	0.26	1.8
Non-intervention	0.41	2.6
Interventionism	0.43	2.7
Interfering	0.5	3.2
Noninterference	0.53	3.4
Interfere	0.66	4.6

to protect the sovereignty of smaller nations." In 2004, Barbados stated, "Trade is a significant factor in the challenge of sustainable development, and trade rules need to take into account the vulnerabilities and the development needs of small States." The Maldives added, "We in small States feel more vulnerable to these challenges and threats, as our security is entirely dependent on the prevalence of global security and the observance of the rule of law by all States. Clearly, the concerns of small States cannot be confined only to the issues of the environment, climate change, sea-level rise, and sustainable development. The ominous threats that are emerging on the political and security fronts of the contemporary world have far-reaching implications for us as well."

Second, along with the sensitivity to the lack of parity, C_1 states are also very sensitive to any suggestions of external interference or coercion. This particular sensitivity to issues of sovereignty stems from their acute awareness and resentment of inequalities in the international system. Table 2.4 illustrates some of the words used in expressing these interlinked concerns.

In 1994, China, Greece and Kenya all emphasized the importance of sovereignty in internal affairs. China stated, "Each country has to draw up social development policies adaptable to its own conditions. International cooperation in this field should adhere to the principles of mutual respect, equality and mutual benefit without political strings or interference in domestic affairs. . . . We are against using human rights as a pretext to interfere in the internal affairs of other countries." Greece reiterated, "The strengthening of good-neighborly relations on the basis of respect for international law, national sovereignty, human rights and non-intervention in the internal affairs of other States is the cornerstone of Greek foreign policy. The implementation of those principles bears particular importance with regard to the relations between Greece and its neighbours."

And Kenya repeated the point, "The Charter of the United Nations clearly underscores that responsibility under the principles of sovereignty, independence, territorial integrity and non-interference in the internal affairs of States."

In 1997, Syria again pointed out this fact, "Among its primary purposes, the Charter of the United Nations provides for . . . the fostering between nations of international relations based on respect for the principle of equal rights and self-determination of peoples. . . . It also calls for non-interference in the internal affairs of States." In 1998, Saudi Arabia too joined in the refrain: "[Saudi Arabia] endeavours to cooperate and to respect the principles of international law and international legitimacy, it rejects violence and terrorism in any shape or form, and it does not interfere in the affairs of others or allow others to interfere in its own affairs." Fiji hammered it home in 2002 after a period of political unrest, "Today I thank the Member States of the United Nations and the United Nations system for their support and understanding during our period of crisis. They stood with us, with words of quiet encouragement, and expressed confidence in our ability to resolve our own difficulties. There were others who were judgmental and strident. Their approach was not helpful. We remind them of the founding principles of the United Nations: respect for national sovereignty and non-interference in the internal affairs of Member States. Countries have the right to seek, and to put into effect, their own solutions to their problems."

Third, the corollary to the sensitivity to disparity and to external meddling is that C_1 states also often condemn the actions of an "other" and emphasize the responsibility of the international community to acknowledge these differences and to take constructive steps to address the issue. Table 2.5 demonstrates some of the words used to convey this sense of entitlement to recompense and their corresponding D_i.

As can be seen from Table 2.5, C_1 states use the word "justice" 1.5 times, "injustices" 2.3 times, "unjustly" 2.4 times and "insensitivity" 3.5 times more frequently than C_2 states. By using these words (along with those in Table 2.3), C_1 states not only emphasize their victimhood to the international community

TABLE 2.5. Selected Words and D Values IV

Word	D_i	×More
Arrogant	0.29	1.9
Unfair	0.31	2
Unjust	0.31	2
Hypocritical	0.32	2.1
Injustices	0.37	2.3
Humiliating	0.38	2.4
Unjustly	0.38	2.4
Unjustifiably	0.47	3
Insensitivity	0.55	3.5
Justly	0.79	6.2

but also invite them to condemn their plight and redress it. In 1995, Algeria declared, "It is only by improving the collective capabilities of the international community to face up to the urgent and most intolerable injustices that a true meaning could be given to preventive efforts of diplomacy, to peace-keeping operations and to the elaboration of a genuine structure of international cooperation." In 1998, Saudi Arabia said, "Developed countries must also allow free and easy access to their markets for the exports of developing countries and must refrain from adopting unjust trade measures that impede the flow of such exports to their markets." In 2003, Madagascar stated, "Personally, I believe that it is high time that the major Powers took steps towards a more equitable partnership. . . . We are far away from the strategic spheres of the think tanks, of the heads of State of the major Powers, and of the chief executive officers of large corporations. In other words, Africa remains the victim of marginalization." In 2004, Barbados complained, "It strikes developing nations as deeply unjust and hypocritical that calls for democratization and good governance in the developing world are not accompanied by calls for those values to be reflected in the multilateral organizations by which so many are governed and upon which so many depend." C_1 states usually close their speeches with the expressed wish that the international community promote justice and cooperation on the basis of equality.

Conclusion

I have shown that one can find statistically significant differences in the public discourse of the General Debate of states that have undergone extractive colonialism and non-colonized states. I have also shown that if this difference in word usage is examined within the context of the speeches, it corresponds to a strong sense of victimhood that characterizes PII. Despite the demise of colonialism well over half a century ago, states still invoke the humiliating memories of their historical past in their public discourse. While discourse cannot be conflated with behavior, it can be reasonably pointed out that discourse, especially speeches made by heads of state in a forum as public and conspicuous as the United Nations, provides clear indications of positions on issues and impending behavior.

We turn now specifically to India and China and use PII to analyze their foreign policy behavior.

PII and the Sino–Indian Border Negotiations of 1960

The long traditional boundary of over 2400 miles shown on current Indian maps is clear and precise, conforms to unchanging natural features, has support in tradition and custom as well as in the exercise of administrative jurisdiction right up to it, has been recognized for centuries and has been confirmed in agreements. It, therefore, requires no further delimitation.

Report of the Indian Officials on Their Statements and Comments Made during the Meetings of the Officials of the Two Governments

The entire Sino-Indian boundary has never been formally delimited and there does not exist between China and India any treaty or agreement delimiting their boundary. The boundary line pointed out by the Chinese side correctly reflects the true traditional customary line of the Sino-Indian boundary.

Report of the Chinese Officials on Their Statements and Comments Made during the Meetings of the Officials of the Two Governments[1]

Introduction

In the 1950s, India and China had forged friendly ties based on a common front against imperialism and the shared interests of the newly decolonized Third World. The Sino-Indian border war of 1962 between India and China brought an end to this friendship that had sprung up between two leading members of the community of decolonized states and instituted an uneasy relationship that continues to this day.

Even prior to decolonization, the Indian nationalist elite had established links with their Chinese counterparts, both in the Guomindang government and the Chinese Communist Party. Nehru shared a warm correspondence with both General and Madame Chiang Kai-Shek and similarly had been in touch with Mao even before the actual establishment of the Communist government. His private papers contain letters from Mao in 1939 thanking the Indian National Congress for a medical unit they sent to the 8th Route Army and their support against "the Japanese imperialists."[2]

In the early 1950s, the India-China Friendship Association was set up with T. Chakravarty, professor of Chinese history at Calcutta University, at its helm. In 1952, a Chinese cultural and scholarly delegation, the first to visit a non-Communist country, arrived in India for a five-week stay.[3] In 1954 the two governments signed the famous "Five Principles of Peaceful Co-existence" or

Panchsheel, and the following year, as a gesture of goodwill, a scholarly exchange program was set up with ten students from both countries visiting for two-year periods.[4]

Despite this initial bonhomie, forged in no small part by similar ideas about anti-colonialism, both countries were born with borders imposed under foreign imperial rule. That the newly independent governments might then dispute these borders is far from surprising, as the logic of PII suggests. The Sino-Indian territorial dispute remains unresolved and, as Prime Minister Manmohan Singh's visit to China in January 2008 underscored, it remains an extremely sensitive issue defining the subtly combative relationship between the two countries. Repeatedly, Indian and Chinese leaders have had to decide to temporarily set aside the territorial dispute in order to achieve agreement on other issues of common interest. The fact that the territorial dispute persists despite this convergence of interests in other spheres serves as a remainder of the sensitivity and durability of the matter.

Most accounts accept that the territorial dispute is explicable as a result of clashing security interests. As both states seek to maximize their state security it inevitably spills over into a battle over territory. Such superficial analysis fails to account for important dynamics of the conflict. Why did India adopt an aggressive military policy when its military was in virtual shambles? Why did China undertake this conflict at a time when it was not only becoming isolated from both superpowers but when it knew it would incur the disapproval of the former Soviet Union? Why did China shock India and much of the international community by declaring an abrupt cease-fire and withdrawal in the concluding phases of the 1962 conflict, when it could easily have militarily occupied the disputed territories? None of these important episodes conforms with the simple logic of security maximization.

One of the last attempts made by India and China to resolve the issue was in April 1960 when Premier Zhou Enlai visited New Delhi for five days of negotiations. The negotiations were a complete failure, with no agreement on any matter of importance. This chapter analyzes the Sino-Indian border conflict by examining both the background to and the conduct of the 1960 negotiations. Drawing on previously unknown documents discovered in the Nehru Memorial Archives,[5] I demonstrate how PII and its dominant goal of establishing victimhood, driving the goals of maximizing status and territorial sovereignty, led to the breakdown of the 1960 negotiations, the last talks between the two sides before war broke out in 1962.

PII explains the peculiar decisions in the Sino-Indian War, including India's willingness to undertake a risky conflict with a weak military and China's decision to declare a cease-fire and withdraw even after it had achieved a clear victory. The case of the Sino-Indian border conflict negotiations also demonstrates that PII, with its emphasis on victimhood, existed in the period just after decolonization, and was not simply a construct of the last decades of the twentieth century. This early emergence of PII is important because it helps us to distinguish behavior induced by PII from behavior that resulted from the shift in capabilities that occurred with rising economic growth following reforms in China in 1978 and India in 1991.

The Sino-Indian Border Conflict

Despite the initial friendly relationship between India and China, the border conflict began to escalate in 1959, and full-scale war erupted between the two nations from September to November 1962. At stake were two contested frontier territories. One was the western sector involving the plateau of Aksai Chin on the western side of the India-China border. The Aksai Chin plateau is bordered on three sides by Ladakh (part of Indian-controlled Kashmir), Tibet and Xinjiang. The other area of conflict was the eastern sector or the North East Frontier Agency on the India-China border near Burma. This sector was north of the state of Assam and comprised the Assam Himalaya region and its foothills.[6]

Ambiguity surrounding the western boundary was reflected in permuting British stances on the border. The British government of India (BGOI) recognized no fewer than three different boundaries in the Aksai Chin area prior to Indian independence in 1947.[7] The northern-most boundary was known as the Ardagh-Johnson line, and it encompassed the Askai Chin plateau within the borders of British India. The Macartney-MacDonald line, however, placed most of Aksai Chin within Xinjiang province, though the Lingzitang salt plain, the Chang Chenmo and Chip Chap valleys were placed on the British Indian side of the line. The third border drawn by the British ran along the Karakoram range, south of the other two borders. Infighting between various departments of the British government, overlaid with tussles between London and the BGOI in Delhi, led to this cartographic indecision.[8] The post-1947 Indian government, however, picked the Ardagh-Johnson line as the de facto border, arguing that this was where the jurisdiction of the Kashmiri Dogra kingdom had ended.

In the eastern sector, the BGOI informally ruled over the region. In practice, local tribes held sway over the area and often conducted raids onto the plains

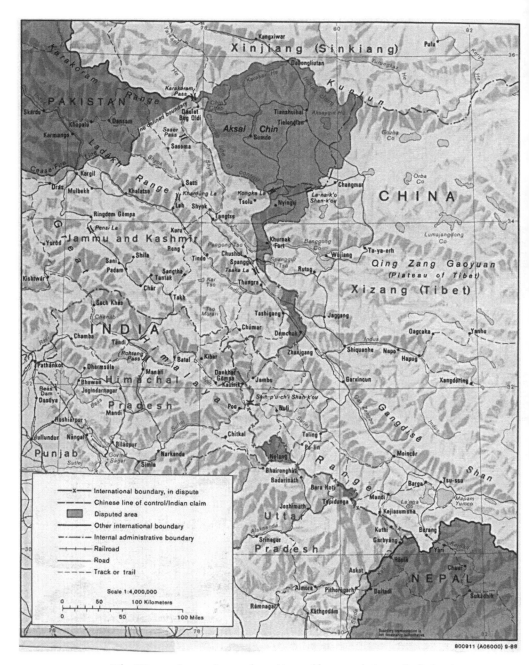

MAP 3.1. The Western Sector. Source: http://www.lib.texas.edu/maps/india.html.

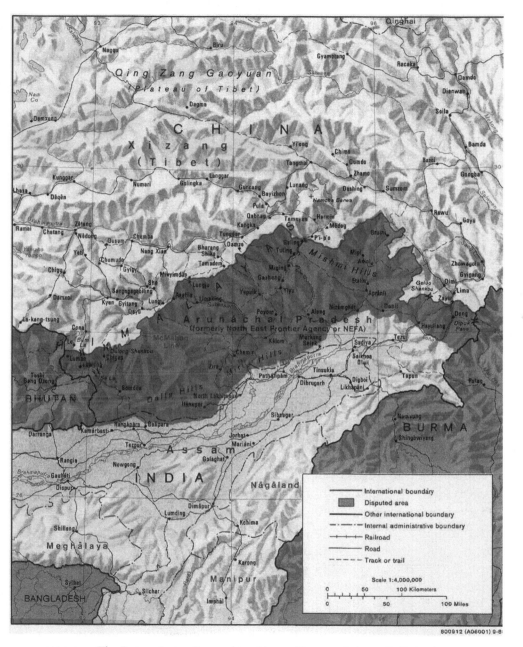

MAP 3.2. The Eastern Sector. Source: http://www.lib.texas.edu/maps/india.html.

below. Around 1873 the British established a series of boundaries below the foothills, and forays beyond them by lowlanders were discouraged. A system of "bribes and punishments" was employed, instead of relying on British presence to maintain control. The territory of Tawang, substantially influenced by Tibet, was seen by the British as essentially autonomous Tibetan land.[9] However in the early twentieth century last-ditch attempts by the declining Manchu empire to militarily fortify its frontier regions caused the British to rethink their strategy. They became interested in establishing direct control further northward as well as maintaining a true border between Assam and Tibet.

In 1914, the Simla Conference, held in the summer capital of British India, brought representatives of the BGOI, Tibet, and the Yüan Shi Kai–led government of China to the negotiating table. The British chief negotiator, Henry McMahon, wanted to ensure Tibet's status as a buffer state and establish an Assam Himalaya boundary. Although the Chinese initialed the Simla Convention they refused actually to sign it, and it was instead signed by both the British and Tibetan representatives—the BGOI took this to imply formal Tibetan and Chinese acceptance of the McMahon line.[10] In the 1930s, however, the Tibetans showed their reluctance to unconditionally accept the McMahon line and give up their influence in Tawang—as a condition for their acceptance they wanted the British to force Chinese agreement to the Tibet-China relationship as outlined in the Simla Convention. Since British influence had been extended into the tribal areas of the Assam Himalayas and into the southern Tawang tract but not into Tawang itself, the BGOI decided to accept the McMahon line in its maps but did not make a final provision for Tawang. The issue was inherited by the Indian government, which endorsed the McMahon line on the grounds that (1) it was not only drawn by the previous government of India but political control had also been exercised there by regional Assamese dynasties for centuries, and (2) Tibetan authority over Tawang was only religious and did not imply any political rights or control.

In both the western and the eastern sector these arguments were rejected outright by the Chinese government, which saw Aksai Chin as a historical part of both Tibet and Xinjiang, and hence of China, and the McMahon line as having been not only rejected by Chinese representatives to the Simla Conference but also imposed on a Tibet that had no right to conduct autonomous negotiations in the first place.

Thus, the Indian government claimed that the boundaries they had outlined in their maps in the eastern (McMahon line) and western (Ardagh-Johnson line, including Aksai Chin) sectors were the recognized and permanent borders.

China claimed that the eastern sector was undemarcated and the McMahon line was illegitimate, while the western sector had never been in dispute at all and the Aksai Chin plateau was a historical part of China (See Maps 3.1 and 3.2).

Alternative Explanations

State Security

Because the 1962 war was a conflict over territory between two regional powers, explanations for the conflict have focused on perceived internal and external threats to state security. Maxwell, for example, argues that the Indian government was alarmed by the flexing of Chinese power next to their borders in the 1950s and adopted territorial policies in an attempt to increase India's influence in Tibet and minimize Chinese authority in the area. Nehru's provocative Forward Policy used physical presence to justify ownership. The success of the policy was premised on the shaky belief that "no matter how many posts and patrols India sent into Chinese-claimed territory the Chinese would not physically interfere with them provided only that the Indians did not attack any Chinese positions."[11]

These territorial maneuvers combined with Indian efforts to shape the trajectory of Tibet. India immediately protested the People's Liberation Army's push into Tibet, deploring the "invasion." New Delhi also decided to shelter the escaping Dalai Lama. All of these moves were correctly interpreted by China as Indian attempts to retain British imperialist rights and influence in Tibet, developments that Beijing understandably might view as threatening. The Chinese roundly condemned what they saw as Nehru's imperialist ambitions. Fairbank concurs with Maxwell, arguing that China's expansionist impulse along the border was "reactive" rather than "compulsive or inbred," and that Nehru's Forward Policy was simply asking for trouble.[12]

Whiting rejected Maxwell's hypothesis that India's Forward Policy was the major cause of the war and instead upheld a more nuanced security argument. Instead, he suggested the Sino-Indian War resulted from the combination of external threats and the prevalent domestic political situation in China. Taken together, Chinese leaders felt particularly vulnerable.

Covert activities undertaken by the United States and Chinese Nationalists, including their provision of support to Tibetan insurgents, stoked Chinese fears.[13] The security threat posed by the United States and Taiwan took place against the backdrop of the severe economic crisis triggered by the Great Leap Forward in 1958. The intensity of the economic crisis precipitated famine and unrest among the Chinese masses and splits within the ruling elite. Refugees flowed into Hong Kong and Xinjiang. The crisis "weakened its sense of control over the populace," and the regime "linked the problems of economic discontent, border security and relations with neighboring countries."[14] In Whiting's narrative, then, India's Forward Policy came at a time when the Chinese government was already feeling intensely vulnerable and prone to react harshly to new dangers.

Beliefs and Domestic Politics

Another set of scholars have emphasized domestic politics and individual beliefs in order to explain the conflict. Vertzberger argued that the Sino-Indian conflict was the result of a clash between the "two diametrically different world views" of Nehru and Mao, legalistic beliefs versus ideological beliefs.[15] Hoffmann also situates his explanation for the war in the ideational realm, though he expands the list of individual-level contributing factors. According to Hoffmann, Nehru and his close advisors, Krishna Menon and G. B. Pant. had a worldview consisting of certain "fundamental psychological predispositions drawn from such sources as ideology, tradition, culture, history and individual personality and idiosyncrasy" that, along with beliefs about India's role in the world as a newly independent nation, led to the clash with China.[16]

John Garver focuses on Chinese misperceptions of Indian aggression directed against its territory. He suggests that fundamental attribution error (the incorrect linkage of particular actions with internal motives or character of another individual) and projection ("transference by one individual onto another of responsibility for events deriving, in fact, from actions of the first individual") characterized Chinese beliefs before the 1962 war. Thus Mao, first, made the attribution error of believing that Nehru wanted to seize Tibet from China and, second, projected responsibility onto India for the difficulties that Chinese rule created and faced in Tibet in the 1950s.[17]

These explanations focus on the beliefs of policy-makers and domestic politics but frame their explanations within the context of state security. Vertzberger, for example, states that China's perception of international law stemmed from its desire to secure its strategic interests. Garver postulates that Mao erroneously believed that Nehru wanted to wrest Tibetan control for China, but implies that this belief and the desire to assert full control over Tibet were influenced by concerns of Chinese security. Hoffmann widens his category of explanatory variables to include Indian insecurity about Chinese "aggression" in addition to historical, cultural, traditional and individual beliefs. If security were the dominant concern, however, any one of three actions would have been more reasonable than those actually taken.

First, rather than undertake extremely risky military action, India should have adopted a conciliatory position during and after the 1960 negotiations. The Indian military was in shambles after partition in 1947. The erstwhile British army had been divided between India and Pakistan. After independence the finances diverted to the military were minimal. The Indian troops lacked both equipment and training. Moreover, the army was stretched thin by commitments to the United Nations in Gaza and the Congo, as well as internal efforts to control the Naga rebels.[18] The glaring truth was that India was in no position to fight a neighbor that had emerged victorious from the Korean War and was on its way to becoming a nuclear power. As the new documents make clear, the 1960 negotiations offered India a way out. Zhou hinted that China would be willing to recognize the McMahon line if India accepted the Chinese claim to Aksai Chin. Yet India, led by Nehru, was convinced of the righteousness of its claim to both territories—essentially swaths of almost uninhabited land not particularly rich in natural resources—and undertook the disastrous Forward Policy after negotiations failed.

Second, had security concerns been paramount, China would not have offered the trade between the eastern and western sectors. The McMahon line was a boundary that had never been ratified by a Chinese government and that China considered illegal; yet Zhou Enlai made clear to Nehru during the negotiations that the Chinese were prepared to accept the status quo in the eastern sector if India accepted the status quo in the western sector. Fravel asserts that in fact Zhou was offering a compromise in order to focus on consolidating Chinese authority in Tibet.[19] But the territories in both the eastern and western sectors border Tibet. If maximizing authority over Tibet were the sole concern, then both pieces of territory should have been vitally important to the Chinese. Certainly strategically both were well located and fortified with natural barriers—Aksai Chin was a barren plateau, and the eastern sector consisted of the high Himalayas. Referring to the Forward Policy Whiting states, "India's minuscule military strength along the border . . . could hardly be viewed as a strategic threat to China."[20] The Chinese were perfectly aware of India's limited military capabilities and, as China showed when it decisively struck a blow against the Indian military in 1962, it would have been very easy for China to occupy both the disputed territories adjoining Tibet and secure its borders.

Third, China would not have declared a unilateral cease-fire and withdrawal in late 1962 if security rationales were dominant. After having made significant and decisive inroads into Indian territory and routed the Indian military, on 21 November 1962 the Chinese government announced that its army would cease fire and withdraw its troops over the next ten days. Moreover, Zhou informed the Indian government that the troops would be withdrawn to its position of 7 November 1959, twenty kilometers behind the line of control. This meant that in the eastern sector the Chinese would withdraw to the north of the disputed McMahon line and then retreat twenty kilometers back from that line, and in the western sector withdraw twenty kilometers from the line of actual control. For the international community this was an astonishing decision. Moreover, from a security perspective the decision was unreasonable for a powerful state undertaking an enormously successful military campaign.

Even if the entire purpose of the strike was, as theorists have said, punitive, during withdrawal it would have been to China's strategic interests to occupy the entire disputed area of the eastern sector and seize the opportunity to obliterate the "illegal" McMahon line. By doing so, they would have essentially been occupying what they had always claimed as Chinese territory, rejected a boundary line that had never been ratified by any Chinese government and secured strategic mountainous terrain bordering Tibet. At a minimum, the held territory would have provided negotiating leverage to allow China to resolve the dispute on favorable terms. In the western sector, which was clearly crucial for them vis-à-vis Tibet, they not only withdrew their troops but they went so far as to withdraw them *beyond* the line of control rather than *to* it. Certainly they had nothing to fear in terms of a protracted campaign from the weak Indian military.

In addition to these strange outcomes, the timing of the dispute is curious for traditional explanations. The Indian military was in an extremely weak position in 1962, and similarly for China the international and domestic circumstances were hardly fortuitous. The Great Leap Forward launched in 1958 had devastated the Chinese economy and thrown Chinese society into upheaval. More significantly, the Sino-Soviet relationship was deteriorating rapidly at this point. Khrushchev withdrew Soviet aid to China in 1960, and the USSR indicated strong disapproval of a conflict with India. Whiting postulates that the combination of the Great Leap Forward and the perceived threat from the United States and Taiwan compelled China to take action against India, but he does not delve into the worsening Sino-Soviet relationship and the logic of balance of power politics. Theories of great power politics dictate that in a bipolar world China should have taken care not to isolate itself further from the USSR. China took an enormous risk by embarking on a conflict with India in the middle of a deteriorating relationship with its superpower ally (a conflict in which the ally had indicated that it would not support China, at the same time that it perceived substantial threats from the United States).

The security framework is tempting because on the surface the Sino-Indian conflict seems a classic case of competing strategic interests—two regional powers clashing over territory in a bipolar world. Yet, as I have illustrated, there were certain significant outcomes inexplicable through a realist prism. The conflict is understandable by applying the PII framework.

PII and the Sino-Indian Border Negotiations

Although the Sino-Indian conflict seems like a classic case of competing strategic interests driven by realist concerns for future security, I suggest that apparently anomalous events in the conflict can be explained only by the PII framework. PII takes into account past colonial trauma and the "wrongs" that India and China felt they suffered under colonialism. These aspects of PII help to explain the breakdown of the 1960 negotiations between Zhou Enlai and Jawaharlal Nehru, which in turn made the territorial dispute in 1962 inevitable. Table 3.1 illustrates each goal and specifically what it meant in the case of the Sino-Indian War of 1962.

Ultimately, PII constrained the 1960 negotiations between Zhou and Nehru in two major ways. First, the emphasis on past suffering and anti-colonialism in the 1940s and 1950s affected both India's and China's bid to become a prominent leader of the newly decolonized Third World. Each emphasized its anti-imperialist credentials and suffering to build solidarity and gain prestige within the developing community. The result was competition and resentment during the post-Bandung conference years that created a hostile backdrop to the 1960

TABLE 3.1. PII and the Sino-Indian War

PII Goal	Behavior in 1962 Case
VICTIMHOOD (Seek acknowledgment that it has faced suffering and be treated as a victim)	1. Asserts it has suffered in the past and is a victim of imperialism 2. Links disputed territories to past history
STATUS (Seek respect or prestige specifically because of victimization)	1. Lay claim to leadership of the developing world 2. Emphasize suitability because of past suffering
TERRITORIAL SOVEREIGNTY (Maintain or gain control of "traditional" borders that are related to memories of victimization)	Assert that 1. it has not made a territorial claim and 2. the territory is an historically integral part of the nation

negotiations. Second, during the negotiations, India and China linked the disputed territories to past history and laid claim to a "mantle of victimhood." Both states competed to emphasize past suffering in order to demonstrate that far from making revisionist territorial claims, they were the victim and the disputed territories had in fact always been historically integral to their pre-colonial nation.

Methodology and Data

India and China are both highly sensitive about the release of any documents on the border issue. In both countries, government documents dealing with the Sino-Indian border are either classified or difficult to obtain, even if nominally de-classified.[21] The documents I draw on for this analysis come from the private Nehru Memorial Archives. The private papers of P. N. Haksar, an Indian diplomat and close advisor of Prime Minister Indira Gandhi, have been released to the public. I discovered among them a virtual treasure trove of documents related to the border crisis, including entire transcripts of the negotiations between Zhou Enlai and Jawaharlal Nehru, as well as top secret telegrams and dispatches between high-level Indian officials based in Delhi and Beijing. I used these documents as well as supplementary interviews I carried out in Delhi and Beijing to construct an analysis of the 1960 negotiations.

Victimhood and Status

In the late 1940s, India and China both emerged under turbulent circumstances. In 1947, India gained independence from two hundred years of British colonial rule, and, in 1949, the Communist Party of China came to power after a painful encounter with Japanese imperialism and a bloody civil war with the Guomindang. They entered a world that was rapidly changing. Not only had the Cold War begun but decolonization movements had gained momentum and new countries were constantly emerging to join the international community. Their size, experience with imperialism and colonialism, and charismatic leaders naturally positioned both countries to lead the developing world. India and China were both acutely aware of their importance to the Third World and strongly believed that their unique suffering had equipped them to act as leader of the newly emergent developing nations. Thus the goal of victimhood drove the status goal of PII to create an awkward, competitive scenario in the 1950s that did not bode well for the 1960 negotiations in Delhi.

The rapid decolonization of the 1940s and 1950s made anti-imperialism the paramount issue for the Third World. As a result, the Asia-Africa Conference held in Bandung, Indonesia, in 1955 made anti-imperialism and anti-colonialism the cornerstone plank of its agenda. Twenty-nine African and Asian countries participated in the quest to "promote economic and cultural cooperation and to oppose colonialism."[22] Partha Chatterjee points out, "[T]he main discussions at the conference were on the subject of human rights. . . . In 1955 at Bandung, no one had any doubts about the principal problem of human rights in the world: it was the continued existence of colonialism and racial discrimination."[23]

India attended the conference conscious of its role as an acknowledged leader in the Third World. As the head of the Indian National Congress, which led India to independence from British rule, Nehru's anti-colonial credentials were impeccable. He believed in India's destiny as an influential world power,[24] and Bandung was the showcase for this. Even though Indonesia was the actual host and organizer of the conference, India was a key player and heavily involved in the details. A letter from Nehru to Badr Tyabji, the Indian ambassador to Indonesia, states:

> I am rather anxious about this Asian-African Conference and, more especially, about the arrangements. I wonder if the people in Indonesia have any full realization of what this conference is going to be. All the world's eyes will be turned upon it. . . . The Conference will represent a historic event of great significance and might well mould the future of Asia and Africa. . . . Because of all this, we cannot take the slightest risk of lack of adequate arrangements. . . . You have been pointing out that the Indonesians are sensitive. We should respect their sensitiveness. But we cannot afford to have everything messed up because they are sensitive.[25]

Even before the conference began, then, Nehru not only envisioned Bandung as the international forum to display India's leadership but espoused a rather patronizing big brother attitude toward other developing nations.

Bandung was the launching pad for India's bid to become a major player and gain prestige in the international community. To begin with, it gave impetus to the international ideology espoused by India during the Cold War: non-alignment. Six years after Bandung, in 1961, the eponymous Non-Aligned Movement (NAM) was established. Nehru's speeches at Bandung, which in keeping with the theme of the conference regularly referred to anti-colonialism and past suffering, also tied his nascent non-aligned ideology to the concept of victimhood. In a closed session he declared:

> Are we, the countries of Asia and Africa, devoid of any positive position except being pro-communist or anti-communist? Has it come to this that the leaders of thought who have given religions and all kinds of things to the world have to tag onto this kind of group or that and be hangers on of this party or the other carrying out their wishes and occasionally giving an idea? It is most degrading and humiliating to any self-respecting person or nation. It is an intolerable thought to me that the great countries of Asia and Africa should come out of bondage into freedom only to degrade themselves or humiliate themselves in this way.[26]

Second, India felt that its role at Bandung was to mentor and introduce China into the group of developing nations. The stage had been set after the Geneva conference of 1954. On his way home Zhou Enlai stopped in India and Burma and pledged China's commitment to Nehru's doctrine of *Panchsheel*.[27] India had already constituted itself as a champion of China in world affairs in the late 1940s and early 1950s.[28] Brown points out that Nehru often "attempted to interpret people to each other when misunderstandings threatened to have dire consequences,"[29] and an example of this was his 1949 U.S. tour in which he tried to make President Truman appreciate the situation in China as he, Nehru, understood it. India was also an ardent supporter of China's entry into the United Nations and campaigned vigorously for that outcome. In fact, India was so dedicated to this goal that it actually refused the offer of a permanent seat in the UN Security Council, citing empathy and solidarity with China, something intelligible within a PII framework but inscrutable under most other theories.[30]

In both the pre- and post-Bandung period with rising hostility between the United States, Taiwan, and China, India involved itself in the Formosa issue and was eager to offer its diplomatic good offices. Nehru exchanged several letters and cables with N. Raghavan, the Indian ambassador to China, expressing his concern about the situation.[31] He sent letters to British prime minister Anthony Eden explaining China's stance on the issue and suggesting a preparatory meeting and conference:

> He (Zhou Enlai) agreed that diplomatic sounding and preparation might precede the decision to call any conference. This could be done by consultation between the UK, the Soviet Union and India.[32]

When China downed two American planes and imprisoned some American nationals, India took upon itself to persuade the Chinese to release them as a gesture of goodwill. A cable to N. Raghavan advises,

> Krishna Menon strongly recommends that without waiting for any announcement from Washington, Chinese government would be well advised to release some American nationals in China, if not all the prisoners such as four jet fliers who have not been tried and, if possible some others also who have received minor sentences. If this is done as unilateral act of grace by Chinese government before any American announcement, it would certainly produce considerable impact upon American public consideration of larger issues. The importance to China morally and politically of taking some such step prior to American announcement would be very great. There would be no sacrifice of any principle or any bargain. It would be pure act of grace and generosity.[33]

After Bandung, a letter from Nehru to John Foster Dulles claimed credit for this act of persuasion:

Krishna Menon returned from Peking today and reported to me about his talks with Chou En-lai and others . . . . [T]he Chinese government has decided in response to our request and "as a first step" to release four of the United States airmen of the Fischer group. I believe this has definitely opened the way to further and final solution of the problem of the United States nationals detained in China.[34]

The PII goal of establishing victimhood with its emphasis on colonial history and past suffering drove the goal of maximizing status for India by aspiring to the leadership of the newly decolonized developing world. Bandung was first and foremost a conference organized against imperialism and colonialism, and the theme of victimization suffused the conference and relations in the developing world in the years after the gathering. Nehru pointed out,

There is no friendship when nations are unequal, when one nation has to obey another, and when one dominates another. That is why we raise our voices against the domination of colonialism from which many of us have suffered so long and that is why we have to be very careful that any other form of domination does not come in our way.[35]

The fact that India thought of itself as crucial to both the conference and the developing world was also clear from Nehru's statements and actions upon his return from Bandung. In a detailed briefing to the chief ministers he proudly pointed out,

The two most important countries present at the Bandung Conference were China and India. Indeed U Nu (the Prime Minister of Burma) pointed out at a private meeting that without China and India the Conference would not have had much significance.[36]

At a later meeting, with members of the Congress Parliamentary Party, he stated, a little pompously,

Inevitably India's responsibilities grow, whether we want it or not. India is in a difficult position. On the one hand, there is no doubt that there is a good deal of admiration for the progress made by India . . . because conditions in all these countries are, industrially speaking backward, they are underdeveloped countries. And so they admired what has been done by India. At the same time, because India is a big country and potentially strong and progressing rapidly, sometimes there is a certain feeling of apprehension against India, a little feeling of, I do not want to use the word "jealousy," but still not liking that "this big country is going ahead fast while we may not be," that type of feeling.[37]

India's aspirations to lead the community of developing nations were echoed by China. China's ambitions to be a world power and regain what it considered its lost status were evident from the time the CCP came to power in 1949. The

CCP's policy of "leaning to one side" did not, in its view, indicate submission to Soviet dictates. It viewed the relationship as a way to secure assistance and enable China to become an equal partner in the Communist camp.[38] In the 1950s, China decided to take steps toward building relationships with the non-Communist developing countries. The Bandung conference of 1955 was the first time the CCP government had gained access to an international forum.[39] It was the ideal opportunity to declare China a part of the community of developing nations and use the conference as a launching pad to increase Chinese influence in the Third World.

China subscribed wholeheartedly to the conference's anti-imperialist, anticolonialist stance. Zhou Enlai's speeches at Bandung not only empathized with the sentiments but also made it amply clear that China felt that the experience of imperialism and suffering was one that it had in common with the other nations present. He repeatedly referred to China's suffering under colonialism and emphasized solidarity with the other ex-colonies. Consequently, in the opening session of the conference, Zhou declared,

> Ever since modern times, most of the countries of Asia and Africa in varying degrees have been subjected to the plunder and oppression of colonialism and have thus been forced to remain in a stagnant state of poverty and backwardness. Our voices have been suppressed, our aspirations shattered, and our destiny placed in the hands of others. Thus, we have no choice but to rise against colonialism. Suffering from the same cause and struggling for the same aim, we the Asian and African peoples have found it easier to understand each other and have long had deep sympathy and concern for one another. . . . The majority of our Asian and African countries, including China, are still very backward economically owing to the long period of colonial domination. . . . We want to do away with the exploitation of backward countries in the East by the colonial powers in the West and to develop the independent and sovereign economy of our own countries.[40]

This theme was repeated continually through all his conference speeches. It was clear from these speeches that, as predicted by PII, China did not consider its atypical experience of imperialism and colonialism any different from or less intense than those of the other Asian and African decolonized nations. In fact, Zhou explicitly declared otherwise and often detailed China's suffering under colonialism:

> Is there any basis for seeking common ground under us? Yes, there is. The overwhelming majority of the Asian and African countries and peoples have suffered and are still suffering from the calamities of colonialism. . . . What some people dislike is the fact that the 600 million Chinese people have chosen a political system which is socialist in nature and led by the Chinese Communist Party and that the Chinese people are no longer under the rule of the imperialists. The countries

in the second group are greater in number, such as India, Burma, Indonesia and many other countries in Asia and Africa. Both of these groups of countries have become independent from the colonial rule and are still continuing their struggle for complete independence. Is there any reason why we cannot understand and respect each other and give support and sympathy to each other? . . . The struggle of the Chinese people under colonialism lasted for more than a hundred years . . . . It is impossible to relate all the sufferings of the Chinese people under the rule of imperialism.[41]

By advocating anti-imperialism, cooperation, solidarity, and peaceful coexistence between it and developing countries with different socio-political systems, China took a crucial step toward improving its relationship with the non-aligned states and building prestige. In coming years it would become an active competitor for leadership of these countries.[42]

To begin with, Bandung led to China's establishment of diplomatic relations with several major African and Asian countries, such as Egypt and Syria, and recognition after the conference from many of the newly independent colonies that were emerging en masse. Immediately after Bandung, China began to brandish one of its chief diplomatic tools to cement relationships with non-Communist countries: foreign aid. The Chinese government saw the provision of economic largesse as a way to be considered a major power in the international system and gain prestige. Aid fostered benevolent patron-client relationships with the Chinese assuming the role of the beneficent elder brother. Between 1956 and 1965, China promised $942 million in economic aid to eighteen non-Communist countries.[43] It was quite a remarkable and grandiose step for a developing country with a tottering economy that itself was dependent on Soviet patronage.[44] Bandung marks the beginning of a period in which China's foreign policy aimed for enhanced prestige often through the provision of aid, elements that were central components of China's foreign policy for years to come.

Thus the Asia-Africa Conference held in Bandung, Indonesia, in 1955 was the international forum for both India and China to raise their profile and increase their prestige among the community of developing nations. In the post-Bandung period this created a delicate situation that would spill over into the 1960 negotiations. China's references to its colonial past and fellowship with the suffering of ex-colonies irked India, and this became a significant factor when Nehru and Zhou met in 1960. India's attempts to "mentor" China and Nehru's consciousness of his indisputable anti-colonial credentials were equally resented by the PRC, while India thought of China as ungrateful for all the friendship India had extended to it. Thus the dominant PII goal of victimhood and the goal of status served to undermine the prospects for successful negotiations in 1960.

Victimhood and Territorial Sovereignty

In 1960, when Zhou Enlai and Nehru came together to discuss the dispute, they were each armed with a list of grievances. From the verbatim transcripts of the negotiations,[45] it is clear that India and China each perceived itself as the victim and sought to have the other recognize it as such. This led both Zhou and Nehru to emphasize the historical significance of the disputed territories, and to dwell on past suffering in a struggle to claim the "mantle" of victimhood. Their stance on territorial sovereignty was intrinsically connected with their concept of themselves as the victim. They were each insistent they had not put forward any territorial claims. Their acute sensitivity to past suffering and insistence on preserving what they perceived as pre-colonial traditional borders made compromise even more difficult to achieve. They stressed the integral status of the disputed territories and were righteously indignant when faced with any accusations of territorial claims by the other side.

At the very first meeting, on 20 April 1960, Nehru struck a resentful tone: "Your Excellency may say that these are [the] territorial claims of India. But when did we make these claims? We have shown these areas in maps in precise latitude and longitude, and this description is before China and the world for a considerable time and no objection was taken to these by the Chinese government since 1949 and even before that period."[46] Zhou responded in kind at both that and subsequent meetings: "[T]he purpose of making this explanation is to show that we have made no territorial claims but that we want to maintain the status quo with a view to reaching a solution."[47] "We have brought in all these historical facts only to show that there has been a dispute for long and that the boundary is not delimited. We did not make any claims nor did we put forward any pre-requisites for talks."[48] "We feel that there is no basis for [the] Indian claim to this territory . . . like this it will be impossible to find a solution . . . we cannot accept any territorial claims."[49]

For the Chinese the issue was very simple—Aksai Chin was an integral and historical part of China. Zhou emphasized this fact repeatedly during the 1960 negotiations. The Chinese fixation on Aksai Chin has been interpreted by scholars as derivative of China's interests in securing Tibet. But it was much more than that. Aksai Chin was seen as historically a part of both Xinjiang and Tibet,[50] two regions of territory considered vital to Chinese unification and nationalization.[51] On the first day of the talks, Zhou stated, "I have pointed out that the main part of the area, namely Aksai Chin, is not under the administrative jurisdiction of Tibet but of Sinkiang. Our jurisdiction has been exercised there not only since 1949 but for a long time in history . . . . It is the main route joining Sinkiang to [the] Ari region of Tibet and this has been so for a very long time."[52]

Both Xinjiang and Tibet held special historical significance for the Chinese. Xinjiang and Tibet were two of many new pieces of territory that fell under Qing control—Xinjiang, Taiwan, Mongolia, Tibet, Kokonor and the southwest provinces all became permanent territorial acquisitions between the late seventeenth and early eighteenth centuries. In the mid-eighteenth century after the elimination of the Zunghar state, the Qing aggressively promoted the colonization of Turkestan and the settlement of Xinjiang. Through a series of coercive and material incentives they encouraged migration and shifted thousands of military forces and agrarian settlers toward the borders of the empire to secure newly seized territory.[53] Chinese scholars point to the influence of the Yuan dynasty as the first evidence of suzerainty over Tibet, but actual military control over Lhasa was exercised when the Qing armies entered Lhasa in 1720 and established a fluid protectorate over Tibet.

Perdue states that the creation of modern China's identity as a "multinationality nation state" (duo minzu guojia) is attributed by the Chinese to these projects of territorial "unification." Nationalists interpreted the Qing conquests and colonization as necessary to integrate China's minorities. Xinjiang ("New Frontier"), for example, was viewed as "naturally" belonging to the Chinese, and its recovery from the Zunghars was seen as fulfilling "a preexisting definition of national territory."[54] Similarly with respect to Tibet, the Chinese Republican government as well as the CCP took the stance that Tibet had been subjugated by the Manchus and was hence automatically a part of the Chinese nation. In fact, one of the major nationalistic goals of the CCP was to restore China to its former glory, and control of Xinjiang and Tibet had huge symbolic significance.

The importance of these territories to the concept of a modern unified Chinese nation was underscored by the issue of "lost" territories and imposed treaties. With the decline of the Qing and the inroads of imperial powers, China was forced to sign a number of "unequal" treaties, and this resulted in a complete rejection of colonial boundaries and a national obsession with "rightfully" reclaiming pieces of territory deemed to have been lost through colonial vagaries. In Xinjiang, China was forced to surrender nearly 350,000 square miles of territory to Russia in the mid-nineteenth century, as well as grant them special trading privileges and the right to station consuls in the region. With respect to

Tibet, treaties such as the Anglo-Tibet Convention of 1904 by which the BGOI essentially converted Tibet into another of its "native-state" protectorates, and the Simla Convention of 1914, which drew up the McMahon line, were seen as humiliations suffered at the hands of Western imperialists.[55] As Zhou pointed out to Nehru, "[This] dispute was left to us by imperialism. . . . It shocked and distressed us that India should try to impose on us the provisions of the secret treaty of the Simla Convention which, moreover, was never accepted by any of the Chinese governments."[56]

The Chinese were indignant at what they saw as India's refusal to repudiate imperialist borders drawn by colonial powers. The fact that a colonized state would not completely reject the arrangements imposed by a bullying power was baffling to Beijing. The 1961 official report of the Chinese side on the 1960 negotiations states,

[As] for the alignment claimed by the Indian side, it does not at all present any so-called traditional customary line; it has neither been confirmed by history nor sanctioned by any treaty or agreement but is a line planned out by the British imperialists for the purpose of implementing its policy of aggression and expansion against China's Sinkiang and Tibet and which only appeared for the first time in 1954 on official Indian maps as its territorial claim.[57]

Zhou coldly pointed out in a meeting with the Indian home minister Sardar Swaran Singh that both India and China had been under the sway of imperialism, but today they were independent and certainly should not abide by the actions of old imperialistic regimes.[58] Thus, for China, the victimizers were India as well as the imperialist powers who had redrawn traditional borders.

For India, the issue was more complex. First, India not only claimed that these territories had been controlled by Indian dynasties prior to the British, but they also saw themselves as the successors to the BGOI, which they believed had simply formalized the more fluid pre-colonial borders and arrangements. Indeed when Nehru referred to the BGOI during the 1960 negotiations, he called it the government of India. For them it was natural to adopt the treaties and boundaries that the colonial British administration had drawn up with neighboring states.

The 2002 publication of India's classified official history of the war asserted that the boundary in the western sector had been "sanctified by custom and tradition."[59] They claimed that the first confirmation of the border was through the 1684 Treaty of Tingmosgang between Ladakh and Tibet. Subsequently it was reaffirmed by the treaty of 1842 between the Dogra ruler of Kashmir on the one hand and the Dalai Lama and the Chinese emperor on the other, which declared that Ladakh's boundary was fixed from ancient times. The Ministry of

Defence history points out here that this meant that the Ladakh–Tibet boundary was accepted and recognized and did not require any formal delimitation. After Kashmir came under the sway of the BGOI, Lord Harding suggested a joint boundary commission with Tibet and China to formally outline the border in 1847, and in 1858 an agreement was signed between Dewan Basti Ram of Kashmir and Mangual Islae of Tibet to again confirm the traditional border.[60] The eastern sector was defined by an exchange of notes between the BGOI and Tibet in March 1914 and confirmed by the Simla Convention (and initialed by the Chinese representative) in April 1914. The McMahon line was not, however, a new boundary but merely "formalized an alignment up to which Indian rulers had been administering as far back as the centuries before the Christian era when were compiled the great Sanskrit epics such as the *Mahabharata* and the *Ramayana*."[61] Moreover the BGOI tactic of traveling in that area and administering the tribal occupants through a series of treaties, subsidy payments and occasional use of force was simply inherited from their predecessors in Assam, the Ahom dynasty, who in turn were carrying on an established modus operandi of Indian dynasties such as the Pala of Bengal.[62]

On 23 April 1960, Nehru gave Zhou a long historical explanation of the Indian position, and his remarks demonstrate that the Indians believed in the continuity of administrative control and borders, from pre-British to post-British, over these sectors. At the end of his explanation he stated, "There is no question of our making any territorial claim, that is to say, any claim on a fresh territory which did not belong to India or to Kashmir state throughout this long period."[63] The Indians thus viewed this territory as an integral part of the pre-colonial Indian empire, and to cede it to the Chinese was unthinkable.

Second, the partition of India and the creation of Pakistan in 1947 were unequivocally deplored by the Indian National Congress. The shock of the loss of this territory, followed by a war over Kashmir that resulted in the redrawing of traditional borders, had a significant impact on India. Acutely sensitive to the humiliations suffered under colonialism, the potential loss of even more historically significant territory was not something the Indians were willing to think about. Nehru declared,

> [A]ccording to us, the boundary between Sinkiang and Ladakh is traditional and customary . . . and can be traced back to the 10th century . . . . [In] 1899, the British made proposals to the Chinese again suggesting that this recognized boundary should be clearly defined. From all this it would appear that till the 19th century there was no divergence of opinion on the alignment of the boundary of Ladakh in the parties concerned, namely the Ladakhis, Kashmiris, Tibetans, Chinese, Indians or the British.[64]

For India, the direct victimizer was China and the indirect victimizer was the British colonial regime. This was because the Indians bitterly blamed British divide-and-rule policies for the loss of Pakistan, making them hyper-sensitive to any perceived bullying by China and to the loss of more territory. The complexity of the Indian position stemmed from New Delhi's acceptance of British efforts to formalize the pre-colonial boundaries.

Both the Chinese and Indians regarded the disputed territory as integral to their respective nations, were outraged that the historical significance of these territories could be misinterpreted as territorial claims and were also eager for the other side to acknowledge that they had suffered injury under imperialism. Zhou reiterated to Nehru that the dispute had been "left over by history,"[65] to which Nehru retorted that no new boundaries had been fixed by the Simla Convention, and rather it simply formally laid down what the boundaries *should* have been.[66] Both sides talked continuously of national feelings on the issue. Zhou, for example, emphasized,

> this [Simla Convention] has been a shock to the Chinese people and it has hurt their feelings because these are the legacies of imperialism . . . . [T]he British tried to use their special rights [in Tibet] in order to split Tibet from China, completely or partly, and it was also in this period that the British coined the word "suzerainty." . . . They brought pressure on China and Tibet to negotiate with McMahon.[67]

He extended these sentiments to Xinjiang as well:

> Sinkiang had long historical relations with China dating to as early as the Han dynasty 2000 years ago, and we have uninterrupted historical records to prove this. . . . We never realized there was any dispute in this area. . . . The Indian government has asked us to withdraw troops from this area which has been historically a part of China. . . . Like this it will be impossible to find a solution.[68]

Similarly, on the very first day of the negotiations between Zhou and Nehru, Nehru had declared, "[T]here is a powerful feeling in India regarding the Himalayan mountains. These are tied up with ancient culture and history and whatever happened, these mountains have always been looked upon as the frontiers of India."[69] The sense of victimization by China was so strong in the country that Nehru had been forced to make an impassioned statement in the Lok Sabha in February:

> It has been said that the Government, and particularly I suppose I, as being the Foreign Minister, have been unfair to Parliament, and have not been quite honest, that we are dying down, we have surrendered, we have submitted to some kind of national humiliation. It has even been said that there is no instance in history like this. . . . I wish to point out that if the Government is charged with submitting to anything that may be considered "national humiliation," then it is a matter of high-

est importance for this House and this country to be clear about. No Government which even remotely is responsible for anything that may be considered "national humiliation" is deserving of continuing as a Government.[70]

Even prior to Zhou's visit, Nehru received a number of letters complaining of Chinese aggression. The president of the Jammu and Kashmir Praja Parishad wrote: "[T]he incursions of the Chinese in our territory are no doubt a challenge to the honor, integrity and independence of India and it is the sacred duty of every individual in this country to accept the challenge and try to save the honour and integrity of our motherland. . . . We expect from you that you will take a firm attitude with the aggressor and will not barter away the honour of the country and the sentiments of its people. . . . You are, we hope, fully aware of the great sacrifices which our fore-fathers made in Ladakh and we hold every inch of this territory sacred and inviolable."[71]

This eagerness to portray their countries as victims took on a bizarrely competitive nature, where suffering was the metric of interest. In a meeting with Finance Minister Morarji Desai, for example, Zhou brought up the fact that, like India, China had also lost to the imperialists and been reduced to the status of a semi-colony. To this Desai retorted, "[T]hese foreign incursions and occupations were confined only to the periphery of China," and Zhou shot back that "it was not so and even at places as deep as Chungkiang a handful of foreign imperialists controlled the fate of China by being in league with the warlords."[72] Desai went on to indignantly defend the Indian position: "[We] have never had any territorial designs on any country and yet we are blamed in China for being imperialists."[73]

Thus when Nehru and Zhou met in 1960, the goal of victimhood played a crucial role in shaping their attitudes toward the conflict. Each leader took pains to outline the historical significance of the contested territory, and each was eager to show that they had been victimized in the past and were again facing the specter of aggression. That in turn influenced their stance on territorial sovereignty: they insisted that they were not making any territorial claims; rather they emphasized that these territories had always been an integral part of their country.

The Failure of the 1960 Negotiations

As a result of PII, the 1960 negotiations between Zhou Enlai and Jawaharlal Nehru failed spectacularly. The goals of establishing victimhood, territorial sovereignty and status ensured a hostile outcome. PII thus explains the three puzzling outcomes mentioned earlier in this chapter.

First, India, despite being in a militarily weak position, could not adopt a conciliatory attitude during the negotiations. Even prior to the negotiations, the attention to status driven by victimhood had created a disadvantageous atmosphere. Documents show that the Indians were hostile and suspicious of China's intentions long before Zhou Enlai set foot in Delhi. After Nehru's invitation had been issued to Zhou, a telegram from Foreign Secretary Dutt to Indian ambassador Parthasarathy in Beijing remarks: "Chou Enlai intends staying here till April 25. This is rather longer than we expected."[74] Another telegram from Ambassador Parthasarathy to Secretary Dutt a few days later a little disjointedly states:

> It is evident . . . that the Chinese want to show that they are most anxious for a settlement and will appear extremely reasonable which does not mean that they will be accommodating or give up in any way their basic approach. Their main line seems to be that the two sides have different conceptions of the boundary which has remained vague and undefined for centuries. There is genuine misunderstanding on both sides which can be corrected by agreeing in a friendly way to delimit the boundary. From this they will proceed to propose a joint committee to undertake the delimitation of the boundary. The Chinese will maintain this posture of reasonableness trying to make it difficult for us to reject their approach. But we should clearly say "no" to any attempt to persuade us to accept joint discussions to delimit the entire boundary or sections thereof. I feel politically we are in a strong position to maintain our clearly stated policy.[75]

Subsequently during the negotiations, India rejected the main proposals put forward by Zhou—namely, a trade of western for eastern sectors and a withdrawal of military forces of the two states from the boundary.

Second, the Chinese had a dual approach with respect to the two sectors. They stated that the eastern sector definitely was disputed territory with undefined and undemarcated borders.[76] As far as the western sector was concerned, however, the Chinese position was that it had never been in dispute. Zhou stated, "As regards the western sector of the boundary, no question has ever been raised in the past and we never thought there was any question on that side. . . . New China has only inherited this area as shown by history."[77] Zhou proposed that the current "status quo" should be maintained. This implied that if the Indians agreed to compromise in the western sector, the Chinese would eventually be prepared to recognize the McMahon line. On the first day of the talks, Zhou declared, "We stated that we do not recognize the McMahon line but that we were willing to take a realistic view with Burma and India."[78] This clear hint was re-enforced during the meeting by his suggestion that

> [we] can avoid clashes and misunderstanding by maintaining the status quo and removing the forces from the border thus making the border one of everlasting friendship. We have made no claims and we have only asked for status quo and

negotiations. . . . We have always said status quo should be maintained. . . . We have advocated status quo because that is the most advantageous thing. . . . When we say status quo, we mean status quo prevailing generally after independence and this would also show the friendliness of our attitude.[79]

A couple of days later, Zhou was even more blunt, "One may then ask, is it impossible to settle our dispute in the eastern sector? No. We take the following position: a) we say that we cannot recognize the McMahon line b) but we will not cross that line since Indian troops have already reached it; and c) as regards two or three points where Indians have exceeded the McMahon line, we are willing to maintain the status quo pending negotiations."[80] The message that China was willing to have a trade-off was made amply clear in further meetings: "[In] the eastern sector we acknowledge that what India considers its border has been reached by India's actual administration. But, similarly, we think India should accept that China's administrative personnel has reached the line which it considers to be her border (in the western sector)."[81]

This was not, however, a compromise on China's part. Rather it was simply the fact that Aksai Chin was considered historically a part of *both* Xinjiang and Tibet—two very important pieces of territory—that drove the Chinese to make the offer. It was true that they believed the McMahon line had been imposed on them against their will, but the territory in the eastern sector (the Tawang tract) was seen as having been *influenced* by Tibet rather than having been historically a *part* of Tibet.

Government dispatches show that the Indians fully understood the hints thrown out by Zhou, but both the western and the eastern sector were seen as equally historically integral to the country. A telegram from the foreign secretary circulated to some of the Indian heads of mission in different countries on 27 April states,

> It is quite obvious that the Chinese aim is to make us accept their claim in Ladakh as a price for their recognition of our position in NEFA (eastern sector). Throughout the discussions they have invariably connected Ladakh with NEFA and stressed that the same principles of settling the boundary must govern both areas. It was also obvious that if we accepted the line claimed by China in Ladakh they would accept the McMahon line. There might be need for minor frontier rectifications but that would not create much practical difficulty.[82]

Third, Zhou also proposed a cessation of patrolling in the disputed areas and a pull back of the military forces of both states. At the first meeting, when he suggested maintaining the status quo, he threw out a hint about a possible military pullback: "[T]he purpose of making this explanation is to show that we have made no territorial claims but that we want to maintain the status quo with a view to reaching a solution and also to take the military forces away from the border."[83] In a subsequent meeting, he elaborated,

> There should be a line between the two areas actually controlled by the two sides. In order to ensure tranquillity along the border, to facilitate the work of the survey teams and in the interest of friendship, we should maintain a distance between the forces on either side. We have suggested the distance to be 20 kilometers but your Excellency [Nehru] said that you were not in favor of it, on account of geographical features. We may, however, fix any other distance which would be suitable to geographical features. Thus, we can avoid clashes between the armed forces of our two countries. This is also for the purpose of establishing a border of perpetual friendship and preventing any untoward incidents.[84]

Zhou repeated this suggestion the following day:

> In order to maintain the status quo, even after the boundary line is determined, we should make it a line of friendship and for this purpose forces of both sides should be removed from the border. The distance to which each force should be removed can be decided by mutual agreement and in accordance with favorable geographical features. Merely stopping the patrolling of the border will not remove danger.[85]

Zhou's proposal during the negotiations was the precursor to 1962, when the Chinese government declared a unilateral cease-fire and pulled their troops twenty kilometers back beyond the line of control. This declaration at one stroke vindicated the Chinese position that they were the victimized party rather than the aggressors in the conflict and enhanced their prestige vis-à-vis the international community. It was also a sharp humiliating lesson to India, which had rejected the option of a similar positioning of troops during the negotiations.

India was not only annoyed by the implication that both pieces of territory might not be equally important to it but also resented the fact that the Chinese gave the appearance of making a very "reasonable" offer that the Indians would be eager to seize. A secret telegram from the Indian embassy in Beijing irately states,

> The People's Daily editorial has generally tried to explain that the Chinese side made proposals for a reasonable settlement of the boundary question but that the Indian side was not prepared for a settlement even though the Government of India itself had at various times put forward some of the arguments contained in Chou Enlai's proposals. While there is no attempt directly blaming the Indian side for the failure of the talks, by stressing the constructive efforts of Chou Enlai, the reader is left in little doubt as to why no agreement was possible.[86]

In 1960, clearly influenced by PII's dominant goal of establishing victimhood driving the goals of territorial sovereignty and status, the Indians did not take a long, hard look at their weak position and rejected any possible solutions to the

territorial dispute. Buoyed by confidence in its international position as a leading member of the developing community of nations deeply engaged in world
affairs, India launched the disastrous Forward Policy shortly after the failure of
the 1960 negotiations. Interestingly, hints of India's misplaced faith in its prowess
could be found even during Bandung, when Nehru bombastically proclaimed
to the assembly, "We will defend ourselves with whatever arms and strength we
have, and if we have no arms we will defend ourselves without arms. I am dead
certain that no country can conquer India."[87]

Conclusion

PII consisting of the dominant goal of victimhood driving the subordinate
goals of status and territorial sovereignty can thus be used to explain the failure
of the crucial 1960 negotiations leading to the conflict in 1962. Moreover, using
PII as the independent variable helps to explain some of the peculiar actions of
India and China prior to and during the war. The goal of victimhood led both
countries to emphasize their past suffering and anti-colonial credentials, and
link disputed territories to past history. The goal of victimhood drove the goals
of maximizing status and territorial sovereignty. India and China competed
to build solidarity among and become a key player in the newly decolonized
Third World community. As a result the post-Bandung years were tinged with
rivalry and resentment creating an inhospitable atmosphere in which the 1960
negotiations between Zhou Enlai and Jawaharlal Nehru were held. During the
negotiations the two leaders competed to assert their past and ongoing status as
victims, while simultaneously denying that they were making territorial claims.
Rather, both insisted that the territories had always been historically significant to their nation, and they were seeking to delineate the boundaries where
they always had been. The breakdown of the talks in 1960 represented the last
attempt at compromise by India and China before war broke out in 1962.

The Sino-Indian territorial conflict is an important case study—not only
because the conflict continues to define the relationship between the two rising
Asian giants but also because it demonstrates PII's presence and importance in
the early years after decolonization. PII with its emphasis on victimhood was a
product of the trauma of colonialism, not the construct of more recent nationalist impulses that have accompanied more rapid Indian and Chinese growth in
the last twenty years. Yet the persistence of PII and the goal of victimhood can
also explain recent foreign policy decisions taken by these two countries. We
now jump forward over three decades after the Sino-Indian War to analyze the
monumental decision to "go nuclear" taken by India in 1998.

4

PII, Victimhood and "Nuclear Apartheid"

Introduction

On 11 and 13 May 1998, India stunned the world with the detonation of five nuclear devices. Global society scrambled to react—the UN Security Council passed Resolution 1172 condemning both India's and Pakistan's test (which had swiftly followed India's), the United States released a statement condemning India and promised sanctions would follow, the Canadians hastily assured everyone that the Canadian-supplied CIRUS nuclear reactor had not been used in the detonation, while others such as Australia, China, South Korea, Japan and Germany condemned the tests and, in some cases, withdrew their high commissioners and ambassadors.

In the midst of all the indignation, there was a key question that baffled commentators—why now? Why, nearly a quarter-century after it exploded its first nuclear device in 1974 and then halted all further testing, did India decide to finally declare its nuclear weapon state status?

India's peculiar stance and soul searching on nuclear weapons was a matter of public record. Espousing non-alignment in the Cold War world, India under the leadership of Nehru decided to take the moral high ground. It led a spirited campaign against nuclear weapons and espoused global nuclear disarmament. The eight-kiloton explosion at the Pokhran test site in the Thar desert in 1974 was a dent in that image, but Indira Gandhi's government referred to it as a "Peaceful Nuclear Explosion" (PNE) and then halted all testing until 1998. In contrast, after the five tests in 1998, Prime Minister Vajpayee modified the official line: no longer Peaceful Nuclear Explosions, the Indians tested "weapons of peace."[1] Even the code names for the 1974 Pokhran-I tests and the 1998 Pokhran-II tests were telling. The operation was called Smiling Buddha in 1974, but Shakti in 1998. The word "*shakti*" is a reference to strength, particularly the strength of the divine feminine embodying cosmic energy and empowerment.

This chapter turns, therefore, to analyzing a significant and contemporary foreign policy decision taken by India that altered its regional and international power dynamics in the last decade. It employs the goal of victimhood, the most important component of PII, to explain India's decision to go nuclear in 1998. It argues that a heightened sense of injury and a corresponding sense of entitlement explains the timing of the decision. The decision to conduct nuclear tests in 1998 was driven by India's sense of grievance against the "nuclear club" led by the United States, which it believed was responsible for creating an unequal, unfair and racist nuclear order. It was aggrieved at what it perceived to be a deliberate and hypocritical attempt to concentrate nuclear weapons technology in the hands of a privileged few while penalizing the many. This grievance was directed especially at the Nuclear Non-Proliferation Treaty (NPT), extended indefinitely and without conditions in 1995, and the Comprehensive Test Ban Treaty (CTBT) adopted in 1996. Both agreements convinced India of the systematic institutionalization of an unequal nuclear order.

In utilizing PII as an explanation for Pokhran-II, the analysis does not entirely dismiss the role of security or prestige, the two most commonly offered explanatory variables, in India's nuclear calculations. Rather it shows that these explanations have been unable to explain variance in India's nuclear strategy (restraint in 1974 versus nuclear weapon state status in 1998) and are *consequences* rather than *causes* of the tests. They do not satisfactorily account for the decision to test or the timing of the tests. Moreover, it incorporates domestic politics by showing that the ideology of the Bharatiya Janata Party (BJP) had a particularly strong emphasis on victimhood.

By focusing prominently on the sense of victimization and its corollary of entitlement that characterizes PII, this episode shows that the goal of victimhood continues to be prominent in the foreign policy calculations of India, more than five decades after colonialism. The role of a victim requires a victimizer. In this particular case the victimizer was the "nuclear club" led by the United States, which, India believed, had deliberately and maliciously promoted a system of "nuclear apartheid." The role of the victimizer is complex—although the United Kingdom, India's former colonial master, is a part of the nuclear club, India does not direct its angst against it specifically. It reserves its

sense of injury for the "club" in general, and the United States as its leader and
the associations it makes with the club and the nuclear pecking order are rife
with colonial imagery.

This chapter describes the history and background of the development of
India's nuclear program, before analyzing alternate explanations for the decision
in 1998. It then moves on to analyze how PII better explains the 1998 decision
than alternative theories. It shows the existence of the sense of victimization
and entitlement in association with this issue by analyzing around 1700 articles
in the Indian print media. What emerges is a striking pattern of repetition that
unmistakably points to the role of victim and a sense of grievance and injury
as inextricably tied to the issue. Thus the newspaper articles examined in the
years 1995, 1996 and 1998 show that the Indians justify their decision to go
nuclear as necessitated by a prejudiced nuclear system. The tests, according to
this narrative, were the only way to smash the nuclear club and gain parity in
the international system. This is in striking contrast to newspaper articles in
1974, when both before and after Pokhran I, there are hardly any references to
victimhood

The Road to Pokhran II

The origin of India's nuclear program predated its independence in 1947.[2] In
1944, the man who is considered the father of India's nuclear weapons program,
scientist Homi J. Bhabha, collaborated with the Tata business family to open a
center—the Tata Institute for Fundamental Research (TIFR)—for the study of
nuclear physics. Shortly after independence, the Atomic Energy Commission
was formed in 1948 to develop the infrastructure for a nuclear program. In
1954, the Department of Atomic Energy (DAE) was created to give further
impetus to the development of nuclear research and atomic energy. In keeping
with India's goal of economic self-reliance, a strong but not wholly successful
attempt was made to keep the program indigenous. Although India had to rely
on some early help in reactor design from the United Kingdom and Canada,
the DAE strove quickly to develop its scientific capacity for full independence.[3]

After the humiliation of the 1962 war with China, India's defense expenditure drastically increased. Immediately after the war, the Jana Sangh Party
became the first political body to urge India to go nuclear.[4] But it was not until
16 October 1964, when China first tested its nuclear capability, that the domestic debate over nuclear weapons exploded. Yet, despite the hand wringing in the
Indian Parliament and press over the tests, and moral and realpolitik arguments

in favor of and against the tests, India remained nuclear-free for a full decade after the Chinese declaration of nuclear capability.

In 1970, the chairman of the Atomic Energy Commission, Vikram Sarabhai, declared that India would keep open the "option of underground nuclear explosions for peaceful purposes" and announced the launch of a ten-year nuclear and space program to build an indigenous nuclear technological base.[5] Thus, by the early 1970s India had developed the capability to conduct a nuclear test. But the political decision to do so was held off till May 1974. Finally, on 18 May 1974, under the leadership of Indira Gandhi, India carried out what it termed a "peaceful nuclear explosion" that it claimed was allowed under Article 5 of the 1970 NPT, which stated that "potential benefits from any peaceful applications of nuclear explosions will be made available to non-nuclear-weapon States Party to the Treaty on a non-discriminatory basis."[6] While the Indian government announced an explosive yield of twelve kilotons, speculation suggests that the actual yield at Pokhran was much lower.[7]

Whatever the actual tonnage of the tests, the domestic uproar after Pokhran-I was considerable and chaotic—the military was enraged that they had been fully excluded from any prior knowledge of the tests and never consulted, bureaucrats and diplomats complained that their government had failed to take into account the inevitable international sanctions, and the scientific establishment deplored the government's refusal to allow further follow-up tests.[8] Thus after the tests, India found itself in the peculiar position of having the capability to build nuclear explosives but no political authorization actually to do so.

For the next two decades, India defied international expectations and did not conduct any follow-up tests until Pokhran II in May 1998.

India Goes Nuclear

In January 1998, the Lok Sabha[9] elections were announced and held in four stages from 16 February through 7 March. The BJP, running on the plank of Hindutva,[10] had briefly held power in 1996 and now hoped to gain enough seats in parliament to form a government of its own, or as the majority party in a stable coalition. The BJP was the political successor of the Jana Sangh, the political party that had called for nuclear weapons after India's 1962 defeat in the war with China. In March the election results showed that the BJP earned 26 percent of the popular vote and 250 seats in parliament, leaving them 22 seats short of a majority. After negotiations with regional parties, the BJP came to power at the head of a majority coalition. The BJP manifesto clearly supported the nuclear option in the face of international pressure, but given the fact that in Indian general elections, foreign policy issues are not significant for voters, it was not on the campaign agenda. Moreover, it was not expected that the BJP, a mere two months after assuming power and leading a wobbly coalition of fourteen fractious parties, would break with years of tradition and take a step that previous governments had refused to take.

On 11 May 1998, Prime Minister Vajpayee convened a hurried press conference to make a terse speech:

> I have an important announcement to make. Today at 1545 hours, India conducted three underground nuclear tests in the Pokhran range. The tests conducted today were with a fission device, a low yield device and a thermonuclear device. The measured yields are in line with expected values. Measurements have also confirmed that there was no release of radioactivity into the atmosphere. These were contained explosions like the experiment conducted in May 1974. I warmly congratulate the scientists and engineers who have carried out these successful tests.[11]

Vajpayee's announcement created shock waves both at home and abroad. As the journalist Raj Chengappa aptly noted, for "a garrulous nation," India was astonishingly successful at keeping its nuclear weapons test preparations a secret.[12] Domestically, while the tests generated controversy and spawned bitter detractors, the general prevailing mood was one of support and pride in India's new nuclear power status. An opinion poll conducted by the Indian Market Research Bureau on 12 May, less than twenty-four hours after the tests, showed that an overwhelming majority of the respondents were enthusiastic about the tests. A full 91 percent felt proud of India's achievement, and 82 percent felt that India should build a nuclear arsenal, while only 39 percent recommended that India sign the CTBT.[13]

The media waxed eloquent about the tests: "A Repudiation of Nuclear Apartheid Policy," screamed a headline in *The Hindu*; "Atal (Bihari Vajpayee) Rides Mushroom Cloud in Great Style," applauded *The Indian Express*; "Nuclear Tests: What a Blast," gloated *India Today*.

Internationally, there was a massive outcry against the nuclear tests. It was a huge embarrassment for U.S. diplomats and the U.S. intelligence community, which had failed to foresee or detect the tests despite the fact that imagery and signals intelligence satellites had recorded increased activity at the Pokhran site. The chairman of the Senate intelligence community called it "the intelligence failure of the decade."[14] Shortly after the Indian announcement, Japan cut off aid to India, the United States announced economic sanctions, the Security Council met in New York to issue a statement criticizing the tests and the leading G-8 countries released a joint statement condemning the Indian decision.

Indian leaders were indignant about the tone of denunciation emanating from the G-8 countries and the United Nations. J. N. Dixit, a former foreign secretary (who would subsequently go on to serve as national security advisor to the prime minister of India), detailed the "pernicious psychological warfare" attempted by Western states following the tests in an op-ed in the *Indian Express*. Apart from the Security Council criticism and the G-8 sanctions, Dixit excoriated Western powers for their charges that India's nuclear devices were not indigenous and that Indian claims of nuclear, thermonuclear and sub-critical tests were exaggerated. He decried Western refusal to acknowledge India's legal status as a nuclear weapons state, and defended India against charges that its tests might be responsible for a new round of nuclear proliferation.[15] Dixit perceived a Western attack on India's rightful place in the global international order, an attack motivated by a refusal of these same states to acknowledge India's equal status in terms of legal rights or technological acumen.

Thus the 1998 tests brought a shocking end to India's ambiguous and irresolute nuclear development, and sparked a proliferation of theories seeking to explain what had finally prompted the country to declare its status as a nuclear power after decades of indecision.

Alternative Explanations

Scott Sagan has pointed out that, broadly, there are three explanatory models for why states choose to build nuclear weapons.[16] First, the security model suggests that states acquire nuclear weapons in response to external security threats, especially nuclear threats. Building nuclear weapons therefore increases national security against imminent foreign threats. Second, the domestic politics model suggests that acquiring nuclear weapons is a tool for political and bureaucratic groups to advance their domestic interests. Third, the norms model advances the theory that the decision to build nuclear weapons is an intrinsic normative symbol of a state's "modernity and identity."[17] Most of the hypotheses purporting to explain the BJP's 1998 decision to test nuclear weapons fall into one of these three categories.

State Security

Structural realists argue that international and regional security threats, most notably a rising China and an increasingly adventurous Pakistan, provided an impetus for the Indian government to finally conduct nuclear tests.[18] Proponents of the China threat theory point to the debacle of the Sino-Indian

War in 1962, the ground reality of a nuclear armed neighbor and statements by senior Indian leaders after the tests. On 18 May 1998, Defence Minister George Fernandes declared that China was India's "potential threat number one," and that China was trying to encircle India.[19] Three days after the tests, in a private letter to Bill Clinton that was subsequently leaked by the United States, Prime Minister Vajpayee directly referred to China as the primary reason for the tests: "[We] have an overt nuclear weapon state on our borders . . . a state which committed armed aggression against India in 1962."[20]

Others point to Pakistan as an obvious and ever-present threat on India's border. After three wars (1947–48, 1965, 1971) India had ample incentive to exercise its nuclear option. Pakistani officials had openly suggested that they had nuclear weapons capability since the 1980s, and the United States had been unable to certify since 1990 that Pakistan did not possess a nuclear explosive device. At worst, Pakistan would test in response to India's move and confirm what India already believed to be true and, at best, it would expose Pakistan's lack of a nuclear option, shatter its confidence and bolster India's security and credibility. Still others emphasize that India was sharply conscious of and opposed to potential external interference in Kashmir, and that a strong nuclear deterrent would guard against this scenario.

In addition to these regional issues, others argued that India had "systemic compulsions" that motivated it to seek nuclear weapons.[21] India was a rising power and the one other state, in addition to China, tipped to achieve major power status. The building of nuclear weapons would proclaim it as a formidable player in the international system and boost its overall security capability, making it a powerful actor in the twenty-first century. Nuclear weapons would be a huge advantage for a rising power—in addition to protection from border wars, it would prevent large-scale military intervention and attacks by existing major powers, and also provide a fallback to major technological advances in conventional capabilities.[22]

There are a number of problems, however, with security explanations of India's decision to test. To begin with, one must consider the international and regional scenario at the time of the tests. This was the post–Cold War era, in which India's relationship with the world's remaining superpower had dramatically improved. In the seven years since India had opened its economy, Indo-U.S. economic relations had rapidly expanded. The prospect of an Indo-U.S. military conflict, which had always been remote, was essentially non-existent by the late 1990s.

India's relationship with China, on the other hand, remained uneasy, but there had been no outbreak of hostilities in the three decades since the Sino-Indian War. If anything, the political relationship had improved since India and China had reached agreements in 1993 and 1996 on ways to set aside the border conflict. Pakistan remained a thorn in India's side, but after three full-fledged wars, ending in an Indian victory most recently in 1971, New Delhi knew that it was in a strong and secure position militarily. Moreover, unlike India, Pakistan had undergone tremendous and crippling political turmoil in the 1990s. On the Kashmir front, Indian troops continued to fight it out in Kashmir, but no longer did the suggestion of international mediation—roundly rejected by India—circulate through international diplomatic circles. And certainly, foreign military interference in Kashmir was unthinkable. Thus, curiously, India carried out its tests when it was in a stronger position and in a comparatively safer world than it had been twenty years previously when it first tested nuclear explosives.

It was also quite obvious that the decision to go nuclear would not reduce the propensity of low-level intensity conflict. This had been amply demonstrated by nuclear powers during the Cold War and post–Cold War period. Thus, testing could not reasonably have been expected to reduce the conflict in Kashmir or increase India's chances of success in confronting that insurgency. In fact, India and Pakistan went to war in Kargil in 1999, a year *after* the tests. Nor does concern over China explain the decision in 1998. Even though the territorial issue remained a sensitive one, had India been responding to a "China threat" it should have done so at many points after 1964, when China carried out its nuclear tests. Yet India chose to hold off declaring nuclear power status until more than three decades after China's initial nuclear tests.

Domestic Politics

The adherents of the domestic politics model argue that a combination of bureaucratic and political elements was responsible for the decision to test. The right-wing Hindu nationalist BJP and a nuclear epistemic community had converging interests when it came to the decision to test.[23] The BJP, having mentioned the nuclear tests in its campaign manifesto, bolstered its credibility with its base and rallied the population to its support by testing, according to this argument. An article in *India Today* pointed out that the tests were "a giant leap [by the BJP] toward dominating the national space earlier held by the Congress, this time without the liability held by the 'communal tag.'"[24] Reportedly, when the BJP had briefly held power in March 1996, Vajpayee had wanted to forge ahead and order the tests but lost a parliamentary vote of no-confidence before he could do so.

In this model, first, too much credence is given to the scientific community. The idea that the scientific-bureaucratic establishment in India had the clout to force the government's hand is simply not plausible. In fact, after the 1974 tests, Indira Gandhi angered the scientific community because she would not accept their recommendation to allow them to conduct further tests.[25] Moreover, the scientific community had been divided historically over the issue of tests, while Vajpayee's personal characteristics as a leader made him particularly resistant to bureaucratic bullying.

Second, the view that the BJP were playing to their base is also dubious. Observers of Indian politics agree that few foreign policy issues have resonance during elections. The issues that *do* gain or lose votes are not only domestic (the economy, caste, religion) but local—for example, elections have been known to be won and lost on the price of onions alone.[26] Moreover, it does not explain why the Indian government under the Congress went to the brink and back rather than testing. The BJP may tout *Hindutva,* but the plank of populist patriotism is not its alone—the Congress has done its fair share to incite nationalist fervor, and a test would, by this theory, have benefited it just as much.

Norms

The norms model is dominated by theories of prestige. India decided to test because of its quest to be a global power and gain international respect and standing. As a successful democracy and home to 15 percent of the world's population, it thinks of itself as a great power in the making. Moreover, it has always resented the recognition given to China, especially by the United States, and been frustrated in its attempts to gain the same stature. Both Stephen Cohen and George Perkovich subscribe to this perception of India as a "frustrated great state," which drove it to acquire nuclear weapons.[27] Vir Sanghvi, the editor of the *Hindustan Times,* has declared, "Indians especially long for recognition from the West, anything showing that they are major players in the world, whether with nuclear weapons, a seat on the United Nations Security Council, Western book prizes, movie deals with Hollywood or top jobs with multinational corporations. There is a sense that we can be a contender. At least we certainly want to be."[28]

Prestige and status are indeed very important for India to pursue in the international system. However they are not an adequate *explanation* for the decision to test in 1998, even though enhanced prestige may be perceived to be a *consequence* of the tests. Right from independence India has always sought prestige in the international arena—Nehru's Bandung diplomacy and the Non-

Aligned Movement were all clear efforts to make sure India gained international recognition—yet India's nuclear weapons policies have fluctuated.

Moreover, at one point, India perceived that *not testing* and taking the high moral ground was the way to gain international respect. Further, the 1998 tests came at a time when the concept of nuclear rogue states was gaining traction. China, its "rival," for example, surprised the international community by signing the CTBT because it wanted to be seen as a responsible great power.[29] India was well aware that testing would invite international condemnation, especially if Pakistan followed suit, as India believed it would.

There are more nuanced variants of prestige-seeking explanations, with Jacques Hymans's largely first-image theory of "oppositional nationalism" the best known of these. Hymans defines "oppositional nationalism" as "a combination of 'oppositional' (a national self-definition versus and external enemy) and 'nationalist' (a national self-definition of having a natural right to independence from and influence over others in the world) understanding of national identity."[30] He posits that Vajpayee's oppositional nationalism provided him with "the emotional motivation to embrace what earlier governments had deferred or shunned."[31]

Hymans's theory of oppositional nationalism is plausible. But it too leaves questions unanswered. Hymans refers to the BJP ideology, but his theory hinges mainly on Vajpayee, who he says made the decision almost entirely on his own, not even informing his cabinet. "Vajpayee, unlike his predecessors, was an oppositional nationalist vis-à-vis Pakistan," Hymans assesses.[32] The basic premise of Hymans's argument is that the *key* to the 1998 tests was Vajpayee—the implication is that not only no Congress leader would have gone ahead with the tests but possibly no other leader from the BJP would have either. This counterfactual is impossible to test, but it can be pointed out that Vajpayee's "oppositional nationalism" should have at least precluded him from being the first Indian political leader to engage in breakthrough talks with "the Other," Pakistan, shortly afterward in 1999. Hymans has noted that Vajpayee's emotions toward the external enemy, Pakistan, were a mixture of "fear and pride."[33] Using his theory, these emotions would not have predicted that Vajpayee's praised "bus diplomacy" would take place or that this conciliatory policy would be his *own personal initiative* and result in the historic Lahore Declaration. Moreover, it was an extremely unpopular move, not only within sections of the BJP but also with the Rashtriya Swayamsevak Sangh (RSS), the Hindu fundamentalist organization that was one of the key allies of the BJP.

Varying alternative explanations, thus, point to security, prestige and domestic politics to explain the timing of the tests. But as I have just detailed, India's security environment was, if anything, more stable in the years preceding the tests. There was no doubt that nuclear tests were seen as enhancing India's security and prestige, but security and prestige alone did not explain the fluctuations in India's nuclear policies or the timing of the tests. Domestic political explanations hinge largely on the BJP's cooperation with the Indian nuclear epistemic community, the ideology of a particular leader, Atal Behari Vajpayee, and its attempt to shore up its base. They exaggerate the domestic political benefits of testing, overstate the clout of bureaucratic actors and cannot explain the broader set of foreign policies pursued by Vajpayee. I theorize instead that India's decision to test nuclear weapons in 1998 can best be explained by the dominant PII goal of victimhood, which became acutely salient in the international environment of the 1990s. Only PII explains why India would test again in the late 1990s after more than two decades of nuclear restraint.

PII and Victimhood

PII distinguished by the dominant goal of victimhood helps to explain the puzzling question: why did India decide to conduct nuclear tests in 1998? This question needs to be divided further into two parts—why did India decide to conduct further nuclear tests at all after 1974?; and why did these tests take place in 1998? Clearly, something had changed in the nearly twenty-five years since Pokhran-I. The dominant goal of victimhood with its corresponding sense of entitlement supplies interrelated answers to both questions.

From the mid-1990s onward, India considered itself a rising power entitled to all the trappings that mark it as such. Declaring nuclear weapons status was one of them. While it certainly believed that nuclear weapons would enhance its security and garner it prestige, the difference between 1974 and 1998 was that it occupied a different position in the international system—rather than considering itself the moral leader of the group of developing nations with prestige connected to the cause for disarmament, it began to consider itself a rising power entitled to pursue security and prestige in a world that was inequitable (particularly when it came to nuclear weapons) and determined to oppress its interests. This feeling was compounded by the ascent to power of a political party, the BJP, which subscribed strongly to this sense of victimization and entitlement. It needs to be clarified here that emphasizing the BJP's sense of victimization is not to suggest a counterfactual—that is, the theory does not suggest that if the Congress Party were in power that it would not have tested. Rather, the BJP party manifesto is very explicit about the idea of India as a ris-

TABLE 4.1. PII and India's Nuclear Tests in 1998

Goal of victimhood	India's decision to test in 1998
Adopt the position of victim and cast an "Other" as victimizer	Saw itself as a rising power entitled to pursue the position in an inequitable system
Justify international action by using a discourse of discrimination	Saw the nuclear order as institutionalized discrimination
Have a sense of "entitlement" to a rightful position	Had a party in power that strongly subscribed to the notions of victimization and entitlement

ing power struggling to gain its entitled status, and the sense of victimization is clear, strengthening the importance of PII as an explanatory variable.

The PII framework predicts the greatest likelihood for nuclear testing in the late 1990s because not only did the BJP come to power in 1998, two months prior to the tests, but the indefinite extension without revision of the NPT in 1995 and then adoption of the CTBT by the UN General Assembly in 1996 had convinced the Indians of the institutionalization of an inequitable nuclear order.

Table 4.1 charts how PII with its goal of victimhood played out in the decision to test in 1998.

The 1998 decision as an expression of PII is even more intelligible in the broader context of India's post-colonial experience with non-proliferation and nuclear weapons. Reviewing that history is the next task for this chapter.

The Great Indian Nuclear Debate: From Moral Leader to Rising Power

After independence in 1947, India emerged as a beacon for other countries struggling to free themselves from colonial rule. As discussed in the last chapter, the goal of the Afro-Asian conference at Bandung in 1955 was to register the opposition of the community of developing nations to colonialism and neo-colonialism, particularly as practiced by the superpowers. Nehru developed the seeds of India's approach to non-alignment at this conference. Eventually, it was to become the cornerstone of Indian foreign policy and collectively express itself in the creation of the Non-Aligned Movement (NAM) in 1962.[34]

Although NAM had a practical goal—that is, to keep India far from Cold War politics—it also had a very strong normative component: a sense of moral authority that motivated its pursuit. Nehru felt that by virtue of India's hard-won colonial struggle, its stance against discrimination and its vision of NAM, India merited a leadership role in the world.[35] This leadership position was attached to notions of morality, persuasion by example and the pursuit of ideals rather than conventional notions of military strength and political clout.[36]

India's views on nuclear weapons and disarmament were a natural extension of this worldview.

There has been some debate about Prime Minister Nehru's exact views on nuclear weapons. Some suggest that Nehru was an inherent pacifist who was vehemently against the development and acquisition of nuclear weapons,[37] while others insist that Nehru was an ardent advocate of science and technology who not only "linked the development of atomic energy to the building of a free and self-reliant India" but also hoped that eventually, a nuclearized India, Yugoslavia and Egypt would counterbalance the NATO and Warsaw Pact blocs.[38]

Whatever Nehru's private hopes of Indian nuclear security, there is no doubt that Nehru made many public pronouncements about the perils and evils of nuclear weapons and was a crusader who made sure that India was deeply involved in the international discussions on arms control and disarmament. Bhatia suggests that this involvement was predictable not only because it was in keeping with the pre-independence tenet of *ahimsa*, or non-violence, popularized by Gandhi but also because Nehru was eager to raise India's profile at important international conferences.[39]

India joined the Global Disarmament Commission, agitated for an end to nuclear bomb testing,[40] attempted to mobilize the African and Asian countries in support of disarmament, and drafted resolutions in the General Assembly to call for a suspension of nuclear tests. Through these activities, India created an international image of itself as an anti–nuclear weapons country that would not, under any circumstances, carry out atomic tests.[41]

As a result of this legacy of Nehruvian idealism, ideas that influenced a generation of Indian policy-makers, India has the distinction of being the only country in the world to have engaged in tortuous public soul searching and irresolution about the development of its nuclear weapons program. Up until 1962, there was virtually no political debate on nuclearization in either the Indian press or among specialists and scholarly journals in the field.[42]

In 1962, even after the Indian military suffered a debacle at the hands of the Chinese army, only the Jana Sangh party explicitly called for India to acquire nuclear weapons. There was no shift in government policy to reflect an altered course of action. Indian prime minister Lal Bahadur Shastri refused to exercise the nuclear option and put the onus on the Western powers to restrict the dissemination of nuclear weapons: "India is determined to pursue the path of peace and to work for the elimination of the nuclear menace which faces mankind today . . . . Equally, it is the responsibility of the great nuclear powers,

particularly the USA and the USSR to think of concrete steps for the elimination of the threat that overhangs mankind."[43] With anxiety in the Lok Sabha
about China's atomic tests in 1965 and 1966, the government declared that the
no-bomb policy was "kept under constant review"[44] and subject to change.[45]

India steadfastly followed "the path of peace" until 1974. On 18 May 1974,
India, under the leadership of Indira Gandhi, tested a nuclear device. The
underground explosion was somewhere between eight and ten kilotons.[46] It is
generally agreed that there is no definitive public account that traces the Indian
decision-making process regarding the 1974 explosion.[47] K. Subrahmanyam,
former director of the Indian Institute for Defence Studies and Analyses, frus-
tratedly states that "there are no papers to explain Mrs. Gandhi's decision. . . .
We can, therefore, only guess at her motivation."[48] Those guesses have ranged
from the shock of the Chinese decision to test in the mid-1960s to the Indo-
Pakistan War of 1971 to the pressure exerted by the Indian scientific establishment to the lack of a nuclear guarantee from the two superpowers. No matter
which explanation or combination of explanations is given credence, it was
clear that, even after Pokhran-I, India was still agonizing about nuclear weapons,
going so far as to emphasize the "peaceful nature" of its nuclear tests.[49] India was
unwilling to lose the moral mantle of leadership cast on it by Nehru.

The contradiction between India's long international campaign against
nuclear weapons and the halting steps it took to become a nuclear weapons state
characterized its approach toward nuclear testing until the late 1980s and early
1990s. In that period two things happened. First, the international environment
changed. With the collapse of the Soviet Union came the increasing irrelevance
of NAM. China emerged as the primary rival to the United States after 1989.
Second, there was a significant domestic shift in economic policy as a result
of which India was poised to offer itself as an enormous emerging market for
foreign goods and investment. Because of the international power shifts accompanied by the economic reforms of the 1980s and 1990s, India's perception of
its position in the international system began to shift.

The "militant Nehruvianism" of Indira Gandhi in the 1970s had led to a
greater consciousness of material power relationships and threats in the international system.[50] But in the next two decades a consciousness of the need for
Indian military strength was accompanied by an awareness of India as an emerging power, particularly after the economic reforms of the 1980s and 1990s.[51]

The game-changing and reformist economic policies that Prime Minister
Narasimha Rao and his finance minister Manmohan Singh initiated in 1991
moved India away from protectionism and on the road to becoming an eco-

nomic powerhouse. India's large population was no longer seen as simply a liability. Nandan Nilekani, former CEO of the Indian information technology giant Infosys, says of the results of the reforms, "[It] is interesting to see how an entire country changed its mind on core beliefs."[52] India's newfound economic strength was combined with the decline of moralistic ideologies like NAM that had fueled its leadership quest under Nehruvian leaders. As a result, in a world that saw the beginning of comparisons with rising power China,[53] India now had a perception of itself as an emerging power in the international system.

The crucial difference between its earlier quest for leadership and this new self-perception was this: earlier, India had thought of itself as a moral beacon for other countries because of its role in the colonial struggle and its subsequent development of NAM, allowing it to "rise above" superpower politics; now, it saw itself as a rising power entitled to a change in rules and norms and redistributions of power in the international system.[54] The world for India had always been inequitable and discriminatory but now it was acutely sensitive to any discrimination that it felt would stymie its rise. And the unequal and unfair world nuclear order, particularly embodied by the NPT and CTBT, was part of such an obstructionist and discriminatory agenda.

Disarmament, Discrimination and Victimhood

India's moralpolitik ideology,[55] crafted by Nehru and faithfully followed by subsequent Indian governments, emphasized its commitment to nuclear disarmament and preached a campaign for the eventual elimination of nuclear weapons. India was, therefore, involved in the negotiations in the 1960s for a non-proliferation treaty that it thought would be in line with its goals. However, when the NPT was finished in 1968, India refused to sign it. There was a fundamental difference between the treaty that India wanted and the treaty that the superpowers wanted—"[T]he United States and the Soviet Union were designing a treaty to stop the spread of nuclear weapons to other countries, while India was seeking a treaty that would, as part of the bargain, freeze and ultimately roll back the production of nuclear weapons that had already occurred."[56] As a result, "[T]he question shifted from whether India should actually *produce* nuclear weapons to whether India should sign a treaty relinquishing *the right* to produce weapons."[57]

Implicit in this question was the element of coercion that India believed was attached to the NPT. This was first articulated by V. C. Trivedi, the Indian representative to the NPT negotiations in Geneva, who proclaimed that the concentration of nuclear weapons in the hands of a limited number of states was "nuclear apartheid."[58] Moreover, pressure applied by the nuclear powers was seen, in a sense, as a throwback to colonialism—as an encroachment on national sovereignty that had been won after years of hard struggle.[59]

These normative sentiments with racial and moral overtones came to be irrevocably attached to the NPT. And the NPT itself would come to be viewed as enshrining the inequity of the nuclear regime, delineating the "nuclear haves" versus the "nuclear have-nots."

To India, the nuclear regime was unjust. Its strictures were the product of a nuclear club, composed of the powers who had nuclear weapons status. The exclusivity of the nuclear club invoked memories of British colonialism and created a sense of grievance and victimization. Even the simple concept of a "club" is intrinsically connected with the history of colonialism in India, when nationalists claimed that exclusive "whites-only" clubs featuring signs stating "no dogs or Indians allowed" were a ubiquitous feature of colonial society—and the fact that the sanctioned nuclear powers, with the exception of China, were all "white" nations did nothing to dispel the image. Even the language used by Indian politicians, writers and the media to describe the nuclear regime had strong connotations of a victim mentality. "Nuclear apartheid" became a very common term used by India to describe the international distribution of nuclear power, as did the "club of nuclear powers" and nuclear "haves" and "have-nots."[60]

India's campaign for the elimination of nuclear weapons became inextricably tied to its grievance about the concentration of nuclear weapons in the hands of the few. If the privileged powers were not willing to give up their nuclear weapons, then all nations should have the right to develop nuclear technology. India's sense of exclusion from the "nuclear weapons club" and suspicions of "nuclear racism" began to color the nuclear debate with greater intensity. By the 1990s, this outlook had come to dominate and eventually subsume its campaign for the elimination of nuclear weapons.

During the 1990s, there were two factors that brought India's sense of victimization to a crisis point and convinced it of the inequity of the nuclear regime. First, according to K. Subrahmanyam, a retired civil servant and influential analyst on national security issues, there was an expectation in India that nuclear weapons would eventually go the way of biological and chemical weapons and be outlawed in the international system. Under Article 4 of the NPT, all parties to the treaty had "undertaken to negotiate in good faith the cessation of nuclear arms race at an early date and nuclear disarmament and on a treaty on general and complete disarmament under strict and effective international control."[61] The NPT was negotiated during the height of the Cold War era and was intended for a period of twenty-five years. The Cold War ended before the expiry of that twenty-five-year period. Yet at the fifth review of the NPT in 1995, the treaty was indefinitely extended without revision.

> There was adequate justification to expect that . . . steps would be initiated to move towards delegitimization, prohibition and elimination of nuclear weapons on a step-by-step basis. . . . What happened at the NPT Review and Extension Conference on May 12, 1995 jolted India. The NPT was extended unconditionally and indefinitely. This meant that the nuclear weapons in the hands of five nuclear-weapons powers were legitimized forever and so also their use. The rest of the international community was perpetually subjected to a nuclear apartheid in which five nuclear-weapons powers had the right to possess and use nuclear weapons while the rest of the international community was prohibited from exercising the same right. . . . The Review and Extension Conference of May 12, 1995 converted a Cold War arms control treaty of 25 years duration into a perpetual nuclear apartheid treaty.[62]

Second, nearly simultaneous with the affront of the NPT extension, negotiations for a CTBT to ban all nuclear test explosions by all signatory nations began in 1993. On 10 September 1996 the CTBT was adopted by the UN General Assembly in New York. India was vociferously opposed to the CTBT and refused to sign it. It considered the CTBT an extension of the discriminatory NPT. Arundhati Ghosh, India's ambassador to the Geneva talks, stated that the CTBT "reaffirmed the perpetuation of nuclear apartheid." The NPT "sought to legitimize indefinite possession of nuclear weapons by five countries . . . [and] today the right to continue development and refinement of their arsenals is being sought to be legitimized through another flawed and eternal treaty."[63] The CTBT "became a symbol of Indian resistance to hypocrisy and colonial coercion."[64]

After the treaty came up for signature in September 1996, India felt its stand completely vindicated and its sense of victimization strengthened when the nuclear powers—the United States, the United Kingdom, France, Russia and China—either delayed or refused outright to ratify the treaty. By May 1998, when India undertook its nuclear tests, the United States, China and Russia had still not ratified the CTBT, and the United Kingdom and France had finally ratified it a mere month earlier.[65]

India's stance on nuclear weapons had dramatically changed since the 1950s and 1960s. In the 1960s when the Indian government had condemned the NPT as discriminatory, there had still been hope of the eventual phasing out of nuclear weapons. The tests ordered by Indira Gandhi a decade later were a clear signal of India's displeasure with the discriminatory NPT and demonstrated that India was *capable* of acquiring nuclear weapons but *chose* not to. It was still the moral leader of the community of developing nations committed to disarmament.

India then moved to a greater consciousness of its position as rising power struggling against an inequitable nuclear regime. In the 1990s, both the indefinite extension of the NPT and the fiasco of the CTBT served to convince it that far from the eventual elimination of nuclear weapons, the international nuclear regime was set up specifically to exclude non-nuclear powers, especially India. In this case, the "victimizer" was the nuclear club of five nuclear powers led by the United States who, the Indians believed, were not only responsible for discriminating against India but also for browbeating India on the issue. In this atmosphere of distrust and victimization, the BJP came to power in 1998.

The BJP Agenda

In 1999, the *Financial Express* mused, "[T]he BJP's 1998 electoral performance, its all-time best, was a telling testimony to the assertion of its ideological identity."[66] This "ideological identity" was the BJP's assertion of *Hindutva,* or "Hindu nationalism." *Hindutva*, as espoused by the BJP, and more aggressively by the RSS, was not only an assertion that Indian society needed to be reorganized along Hindu cultural norms but a belief in the concept of *shakti* as key to any revival of India's past glory.[67] *Shakti*, which can be very loosely translated as "strength," is drawn from the Vedic reference to cosmic energy and implies empowerment. The meaning of such an emphasis on strengthening and empowering the nation is, of course, the belief that India *needed* to be strengthened and empowered, that greatness had been lost and needed to be recovered. In short, a strong consciousness of victimhood.

A sense of victimization permeated the 1998 BJP election manifesto. Chapter 1, an introduction to the BJP vision and way, stated:

> The BJP shares, embodies and energizes the vision of every patriotic Indian to see our beloved country emerge as a strong, prosperous and confident nation, occupying her rightful place in the international community , . . . It is a vision to see India, the world's oldest cradle of civilization, transform itself yet again into a benign global power, contributing her material, intellectual, cultural and spiritual energies to change the paradigm at the global level.[68]

The consciousness of victimhood was particularly evident in its exposition of India's foreign policy (Chapter 7) and what its role in the world ought to entail:

> We see a renewed tendency by some big powers to dominate and to impose con-
> ditionalities to advance their political and economic interest even if it is detrimental
> to others. . . . This demands that India's national interest must be protected and
> pursued more vigorously. . . . In the recent past we have seen a tendency to bend
> under pressure. This arises as much out of ignorance of our rightful place and role in
> world affairs as also from a loss of national self-confidence and resolve. A nation as
> large and capable as ourselves must make its impact felt on the world arena. A BJP
> Government will demand a premier position for the country in all global fora.[69]

The BJP's stance on what India's nuclear policy should be was a natural
extension of its belief that India had been coerced in the past and needed to
reassert itself in the international arena. It was acutely sensitive to the pressure
exerted by the entrenched and hegemonistic nuclear regime, exemplified by the
NPT and CTBT. It vocally and colorfully denounced the regime and its tactics
in its manifesto:

> The BJP rejects the notion of nuclear apartheid and will actively oppose attempts
> to impose a hegemonistic nuclear regime. . . . We will not be dictated to by any-
> body in matters of security requirements and in the exercise of the nuclear option.
> We will pursue our national goals and principles steadfastly. . . . [Our goals are]
> to give India a role and position in world affairs commensurate with its size and
> capability, to promote sovereign equality among nations. The BJP rejects all forms
> of political and economic hegemonism and is committed to actively resisting
> such effort, to place relations with the USA on a more even keel based on mutual
> respect, shared values and congruence of interests.[70]

As discussed before, India already perceived the nuclear regime as inequitable,
and both the indefinite extension of the NPT and its vehement opposition to
the CTBT created the uneasy conditions under which the BJP came to power.
As its manifesto made amply clear, the BJP strongly subscribed to this sense of
injustice. When Operation Shakti was launched, Vajpayee exulted in his first
interview to the press: "The greatest meaning of these tests is that they have
given India *shakti*, they have given India strength and they have given India
self-confidence."[71]

Methodology and Data

Government papers on India's nuclear tests, and indeed India's entire nuclear
program, are shrouded in secrecy. Most analysts of India's nuclear development
have therefore had to rely extensively on either interviews or secondary sources
to draw conclusions about the tests. To gauge Indian opinion on the nuclear
regime in general and on India's nuclear tests in particular, I turned to a prominent daily newspaper, the *Indian Express*. Established in 1931, the *Indian Express*

is one of India's most respected and highest-circulating English-language dailies that is published in all major cities.

The analysis I have presented above argues that the dominant goal of victimhood that characterizes PII drove India's decision to test in 1998. To demonstrate this, I searched four years of the *Indian Express* for any and all articles pertaining to nuclear weapons, the nuclear regime, and India's nuclear program. These years were 1974, 1995, 1996 and 1998 (up until a couple of weeks after the May 1998 tests), yielding a total of 1,622 articles for analysis. These articles included reports, op-eds, editorials, letters to the editor and political analyses. Articles that were on the nuclear regime or nuclearization but contained no explicit reference to India in any way or were entirely statements by foreign leaders or intellectuals were thrown out. The remaining articles were then coded for references to victimization.

Before I explain what a reference to victimization looks like, it is necessary to explain why those particular years were chosen. The year of Pokhran I, 1974, was chosen to provide a contrast to the years 1995, 1996 and 1998. PII shows that in the two decades after the 1970s, India's position and perception of itself in the international system changed. Thus, in 1974, India's nuclear tests were *not* driven by any sense of victimization. A sense of grievance about the inequitable nuclear regime emerged later. Thus, the articles from 1974 were not expected to show victimhood. The year the NPT was extended indefinitely, 1995, and the year of the CTBT opening for signature, 1996, were chosen because both of these treaties were key to India's rage against the inequities of the nuclear system. The year India conducted Operation Shakti, 1998, was also chosen, and articles were selected up through late May of that year. This latter period (1995, 1996, 1998) containing the run-up to, reports of, and initial reactions to the nuclear tests were expected to show India's strong sense of victimization. Figure 4.1 shows the distribution of articles referring to victimhood and nuclearization across all four years.

As is clear from the graph, in the 1990s there was a spike in articles referring to victimization in the context of the nuclear issue. How does an article show references to victimization? There are obviously certain words associated with a sense of victimization, such as humiliation, inequity, unjust, unfair, etc. However, a mere search for the existence of these words does not serve much purpose. After all, India could be asserting that the nuclear order is NOT unjust, unfair or inequitable. Thus, rather than search for specific words, each article was read carefully for certain references. Some are listed below:

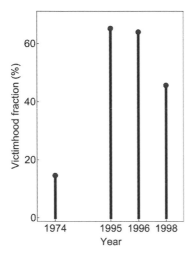

FIG. 4.1. Victimhood Graph.
Source: *Indian Express*.

- The U.S./"the West"/the nuclear club hindering India's quest for nuclear weapons or technology, including through the NPT and CTBT;
- The U.S./"the West"/the nuclear club following a hypocritical policy, either in generally treating nuclear/non-nuclear states differently or treating China as a special case despite its nuclear arsenal;
- India's *right* to nuclear technology and/or refusal to have terms dictated to it; and
- India's sensitivity to any hints of pressure or coercion.

Having read thousands of articles, I would find it difficult to categorize in detail all the numerous ways in which a sense of victimhood is portrayed. But in general, a statement that indicates a sense of victimization shows dissatisfaction with the existing nuclear regime, an awareness and resentment of any effort by nuclear powers to keep India from having weapons, a sense that India is entitled to nuclear weapons state status and an indignation with the hypocrisy of the nuclear powers club.

As is clear from Figure 4.1, 1974 overwhelmingly did not show a sense of victimization. In the months before Operation Smiling Buddha, there was not too much concern shown in the articles about nuclearization or the nuclear order. References centered mostly around the Cold War. There was concern about the superpowers carrying out nuclear tests in the Indian Ocean,[72] worry that superpower rivalry in the region would affect Indian security,[73] and a couple of isolated calls for India to manufacture nuclear arms because of Pakistan.[74] Frankly, there were few articles on nuclearization before the nuclear tests.

After India tested in May 1974, the number of articles on the issue increased dramatically, but there were still very few references to victimhood. There was quite obviously pride in the tests,[75] and a belief that they would garner India prestige,[76] but the feeling that India had a right to nuclear tests and, by testing, had shattered the glass ceiling imposed by the nuclear club was missing. In fact, unlike in the later years examined, reports and editorials examined the international political fallout from the tests but said nothing about the hypocrisy of the established nuclear powers and concluded that the United States was upset because of the damage to its preferred balance of power in the region.[77] Even any references to pressure on India were placed within the context of the Cold War rather than pressure by the nuclear club.[78] There were certainly some references to victimhood with talk of the "discriminatory NPT,"[79] a consciousness of the domination of the nuclear powers and the change in India's fortunes,[80] but these were few and far between.

This tone completely changed in the 1990s. To begin with, nuclearization and the nuclear regime were topics that came up quite frequently before India finally tested in May 1998. So 1995, 1996 and the months leading up to the tests in 1998 were replete with articles discussing the issue. In 1995, discussion was centered mainly on the extension of the NPT and issues related to it. Here there were myriad references that indicated India's sense of victimization vis-à-vis the nuclear regime. The NPT was denounced as discriminatory,[81] as perpetuating nuclear hegemony and nuclear apartheid,[82] and as a tool of U.S. pressure.[83]

In 1996, the CTBT dominated the news articles on nuclearization and nuclear policy. Again, references to discrimination,[84] and even more overwhelmingly, to unfair pressure on India abounded.[85] The culprit was not just the United States exerting relentless pressure on India but the nuclear club in general, including the United Kingdom, and much to India's indignation, even Russia.[86]

This pattern continued in 1998, but most articles on the nuclear issue were concentrated in May after the tests take place. Again while prestige was clearly a concern and there were references to India's security, there were also continued references to victimization. Primarily, the emotion that comes through from the articles was that India had succeeded in smashing the inequitable nuclear order and would no longer be subject to unfair pressure. An article states, "[T]he three nuclear tests today irrevocably give India greater leverage in its relations with the world powers by catapulting it out of the category of 'nuclear threshold states' and into the exclusive club of nuclear states."[87] Another states, "India keeps getting pushed around by any country in a mood to bully. . . . That is the feeling in the field. . . . After years of political and bureaucratic decay in India, there was finally something which made one feel that India did after all have a spine, and maybe after all these years as a 'could have been' the country might actually be in a position to look up and see that sun shining beatifically over it."[88] The pressure on India to sign the CTBT is even directly cited as the reason for the tests.[89]

There are also passionate references to the hypocrisy of the West not only with regard to the CTBT but also in denouncing India's tests and imposing sanctions.[90] A particularly colorful editorial states, "India, the latest nuclear bogeyman on the international stage is getting moral punches from elsewhere also. . . . It is a display of vacuous morality wrapped in economic punishment. India doesn't deserve this, this vindictive diplomacy of demonization. India is not Pyongyang or Baghdad. It is not into the art of nuclear blackmail. It is not steeped in paranoia. It is as the 'disappointed' Clinton rightly says, 'a vibrant democracy.' This vibrancy counterbalances the vibrations from Pokhran. Bill Clinton, with his eyes set on history and his feet on the shifting sands of diplomatic hypocrisy, is too nervous about his own historical burden to see this Indian dualism of national assertion and democratic awareness."[91]

Thus, as PII would predict, there is a striking difference in Indian discourse between 1974 and in the 1990s until the tests in May 1998. It is not that there are no references to Indian security or prestige in either timeframe. It is that whether there are references to security or prestige or not, the majority of the articles make references that can be categorized as emblematic of victimhood. In a realist world, such references would be unnecessary. Security would be all the justification a state needs. But that clearly does not play out in the pages of the *Indian Express*.

Conclusion

This chapter has focused on the PII and the dominant goal of victimhood to explain why India decided to declare nuclear weapons state status and why it did so in 1998. It has used thousands of articles in the *Indian Express* to show there was a distinct discrepancy between 1974 and 1995, 1996 and 1998 in how the nuclear order and India's role in it was perceived. By the 1990s, India's perception of its role and entitlement in the international system had changed—it perceived itself as a rising power entitled to all the trappings that came with the position, including overturning an unjust and unfair nuclear order. It saw the inequitable nuclear order institutionalized through the indefinite extension of the NPT in 1995 and the drafting of the CTBT in 1996, and it was highly resentful of the pressure put on it by the nuclear club to sign both. This resentment and sense of injury was particularly highlighted when the BJP came to power in 1998 with its campaign manifesto emphasizing the inequity of the nuclear regime and the suffering of India. While enhanced prestige and security were consequences of the nuclear tests, they do not explain the timing of the tests or even the decision to test at all. The lens of PII sheds light on both these aspects of the 1998 tests.

How do PII and the goal of victimhood affect China in the contemporary era, well over five decades after it underwent its "semi-colonial" experience? We turn now to China's bitter opposition to Japan's entry into the UN Security Council as a permanent member as a case study.

5

PII, Victimhood and Sino-Japanese Hostility

Introduction

China's relationship with Japan is both peculiar and fraught. On one hand, Japan is China's second largest trading partner with Japan-China bilateral trade valued at $217 billion by the end of 2010.[1] On the other, this strong economic relationship stands in striking contrast to the widespread, and sometimes virulent, anti-Japanese sentiment that exists in China. More so than China's relationships with the United States, the European Union, Russia or India, its complicated bilateral relationship with Japan carries with it difficult and sensitive historical memories.

China's unique relationship with Japan stems from the long history that the two countries share. Japan, once a vassal state of imperial China, subjugated and humiliated the Chinese not once but twice in different periods of time—in the late 1800s and again, in the 1930s. It would be impossible to undertake any analysis of Sino-Japanese relations without taking into account the importance of this history to the Chinese.

Japan's domination and exploitation of China falls under the "century of humiliation" (*bainian guochi*) in the Chinese historical narrative. This term is used by the Chinese to refer collectively to the colonial subjugation of their country by Western powers and Japan. The suffering at the hands of Japan was particularly shocking and remains hugely sensitive, not only because Japan was considered an inferior vassal state at the beginning of this tumultuous period but also because modern Japan is seen as unremorseful of the atrocities that it inflicted on China.

The Chinese government's attitude toward the Japanese has vacillated between active hostility and tolerant amicability, and at different times it has either promoted or attempted to rein in anti-Japanese sentiments in the Chinese population.[2] However, whether because of government propaganda, school textbooks or memories and stories passed down by survivors, anti-Japanese feelings are deep-rooted in the Chinese population and are a key component of rising Chinese nationalism. Sino-Japanese relations have been normalized for more than three decades, but anti-Japanese feelings, while not a new phenomenon, have been rapidly increasing—expressions of it are both more aggressive and frequent.[3] This widespread hostility stemming from the "history problem" (*lishi wenti*) has often come back to haunt the Chinese government and constrains its relationship with Japan.[4] As a result, China often paints Japan as the victimizer and itself as the victim in their bilateral dealings.

This chapter, therefore, uses the goal of victimhood, the most important component of PII, to analyze China's opposition to Japan's bid to enter the UN Security Council as a permanent member in 2004. The issue of Japan's permanent membership in the Security Council triggered anti-Japanese mass riots throughout China. China's opposition to Japan's entry and the subsequent riots in 2005 led to the lowest point in Sino-Japanese relations in more than three decades.

Using hundreds of articles in the Chinese print media (both official and popular), this chapter shows that China's view of itself as a victim of Japanese aggression and belief that Japan has not adequately recognized or apologized for China's past suffering led it to oppose Japan's permanent membership. The role of a victim requires a victimizer. In this case, Japan's image as victimizer is directly drawn from China's memory of the "century of humiliation" in which China was subjugated and semi-colonized by Japan and the Western powers.

This chapter first describes the events leading up to the April 2005 anti-Japanese riots before analyzing alternate explanations for China's opposition to Japan's permanent membership in the UN Security Council. It then moves on to discuss the fraught history of Sino-Japanese relations, and the role of PII and the goal of victimhood. It then proceeds to discuss an extensive survey of Chinese language media that I undertook to assess the narrative choices, attitudes, arguments and opinions associated with the Chinese position in 2004 and 2005. The articles reveal that the Chinese rarely discuss the issue of Japan's entry into the Security Council without emphasizing China's role as victim and Japan's inadequate remorse as victimizer.

Not only do the Chinese strongly resent the brutalization they suffered at Japanese hands and believe that the Japanese show little remorse for their actions, but they frequently and carefully remind other countries of these facts, in keeping with the dominant goal of PII—to be recognized and empathized with as a victim. As I will show, when the issue of Japan's permanent membership in the UN Security Council arose, a sense of victimhood stemming from specific grievances about Japan's colonial legacy in China drove government hostility to Japan's bid. This official hostility crystallized into outright opposition to the bid, and it was backed up by violent displays of anti-Japanese public opinion in China.

Japan's Entry into the UN Security Council

In 2003, a special panel of the United Nations met to evaluate reforms to the organization. In particular, in an era of global conflict, the panel considered ways to improve the effectiveness of the Security Council. One of the reforms they proposed to study was that the Security Council's permanent members be extended to include, among other countries,[5] Japan. This was an eminently plausible suggestion: Japan was the largest aid and reconstruction donor to the United Nations,[6] and it contributed a full 19 percent of the UN budget.[7] In November 2004, after Japan, Germany, Brazil and India had formally declared their aspirations for an expanded Security Council, the panel's report was made public. Its most striking recommendation was two alternative options for the enlargement of the Security Council from fifteen to twenty-four members— one would add six new permanent members as well as three new two-year members; the other would create a new tier of eight semi-permanent members chosen for renewable four-year terms and one additional two-year term seat to the existing ten.[8]

It was quickly evident that in order for the reforms to succeed a key question would be "how China perceived bids for permanent memberships by its Asian rivals, India and Japan."[9] Although Beijing had in the past declared that it supported the principle of Security Council enlargement based on the interests of developing countries and more equitable geographic representation, it had never actually expressed support for any particular country.[10] This began to change in 2002 when President Jiang Zemin first offered support for the inclusion of Germany and Brazil. However, China refrained from endorsing either India's or Japan's bid.[11] Until the recommendations of the panel were made public, its position on India was ambiguous and its position on Japan was slightly more explicit.

Chinese academic Jin Xide summarized the multifold position of China's Ministry of Foreign Affairs. First, China would understand Japan's desire to play a greater role in international affairs if Japan undertook the correct attitude toward its "history problem" (*lishi wenti*). Second, the UN Security Council should not be organized according to the amount of dues a member country pays. Third, the UN Security Council should include more representatives from developing countries. Fourth, China had not yet declared requirements specific to which members should be added, despite these general principles. Fifth, and finally, Japan must secure approval of all five permanent members as well as two-thirds of the UN member countries in order to secure permanent membership.[12]

However, based on the panel's report in April 2005, when UN secretary-general Kofi Annan proposed to expand the Security Council to twenty-four members by the end of the year, China's response was swift and its position had changed from that detailed by Jin. China's ambassador to the United Nations, Wang Guangya, emphasized that the decision to expand the council could be taken only if there were a unanimous vote in the 191-member General Assembly. This meant that a single UN member could effectively reject permanent membership.[13] The issue of Japanese membership also began to gain momentum and publicity in China.

Within days, Internet petitions on three major Chinese Internet portals—Sina, Sohu and Netease—opposing Japan's bid had gained more than 10 million signatures.[14] Shortly thereafter, the Japanese Ministry of Education issued its list of approved textbooks for the year, which included a controversial history textbook glossing over Japanese atrocities during the second Sino-Japanese War. Anti-Japanese emotions were already running high over the Security Council reform proposal, and the textbook controversy fed the flame. Riots and demonstrations erupted all over China. On 9 April a crowd of ten thousand protested in Beijing demanding a rejection of Japan's bid, and among other things, a boycott of all Japanese goods.[15] Similar demonstrations and acts of violence expanded to other cities, including breaking the windows of Japanese consulates, vandalizing Japanese-owned restaurants and stores and attacking Japanese citizens. The *Guardian* newspaper carried a vivid account of the backlash, labeling it "one of the biggest displays of people power that China has seen since the protests in Tiananmen Square in 1989":[16]

> Some were singing the national anthem, others chanted anti-Japanese insults and vowed to defend China with their lives. A few wore T-shirts emblazoned with the blood-splattered face of Japanese Prime Minister Junichiro Koizumi. Many handed out leaflets with a list of Japanese products to be boycotted. Banners called on

Tokyo to face up to its wartime atrocities and give up islands that the two countries are both claiming. One slogan, however, was to prove particularly prescient: "When the Chinese people get angry, the result is always big trouble."[17]

The protests had the obvious support of the Chinese government. At this point, Premier Wen Jiabao weighed in on the dispute by explicitly declaring that Japan could never become a permanent member of the UN Security Council until it took responsibility for its wartime aggression and earned the respect of the people of Asia.[18] Wen's remarks were made during an official visit to India where he stated, "Only a country that respects history, takes responsibility for history and wins over the trust of peoples in Asia and the world at large can take greater responsibilities in the international community."[19] At the same time, as I will elaborate later, he offered Chinese support for India's bid for a permanent membership.

Wen's pronouncement was a startling indication of how China, faced with the very real possibility of UN Security Council enlargement and supported by strong public anti-Japanese sentiment, was acutely sensitive about Japan's bid to become a permanent member and made explicit its hostility to the idea. It led to a hasty and unsuccessful visit by the Japanese foreign minister, Nobutaka Machimura, to China to sort out the issue. His demand for an apology by China for the damage caused to Japanese property and citizens was rejected by the Chinese government. On the contrary, the Chinese position, as Wen pointed out, was that the anti-Japanese emotions should prompt "deep and profound reflections" in Japan.[20] In another attempt to ease the situation, Prime Minister Junichiro Koizumi offered a "heartfelt apology" for the "tremendous damage and suffering" Japan had inflicted in the past on its Asian neighbors.[21] But a specially arranged meeting, on the fringe of an Asian-African summit, between Chinese president Hu Jintao and Koizumi, failed to defuse the situation. Hu insisted that to show its sincerity Japan needed to back up its apologies with concrete actions.

The April incidents sparked by the Security Council issue dealt a sobering blow to Sino-Japanese relations and were described by the Chinese as "the most serious problem in bilateral relations since China and Japan established diplomatic relations in 1972."[22] Before analyzing the role of PII in this issue, it is important first to examine possible alternative explanations for China's implacable hostility to Japan's bid.

Alternative Explanations

State Security

China's relationship with Japan has been cyclical since their rapprochement in the 1970s. Periods of cordiality have been interrupted by episodes of conflict.[23] This pattern is often explained as a result of China's insecurity vis-à-vis Japan. According to Wu Xinbo, China is uncomfortable with the security aspect of bilateral relations with Japan. He points out three major Chinese concerns: the potential Japan possesses to become a significant military power, the "hidden agenda" of the U.S.-Japan alliance to contain the rise of China and the possibility that a U.S.-Japan security alliance might expand to include Taiwan.[24]

Moreover, the Chinese academic literature historically has held the theory that Japan's remilitarization was inevitable.[25] Despite polling evidence showing that the Chinese public "appear not to be too worried about the revival of Japanese militarism,"[26] the Chinese elite believe that Japan not only has a militaristic strategic culture and wants to restrain China's rising influence but also actively seeks to foment conflict between the United States and China, and will eventually develop nuclear weapons.[27] This pessimistic assessment has been underlined by Jennifer Lind, who argues in a 2004 article that current analyses "greatly underestimate Japanese military power."[28] She argues that in terms of aggregate defense spending (corrected for purchasing power parity, or PPP), Japan ranks number three in the world (ahead of China but behind the United States and Russia) in total defense spending.[29] Thus Japan's bid to become a permanent member of the UN Security Council is, security theorists would argue, naturally understood by China as a further step toward Japan's gaining the status of a military power.

If, in fact, China's preoccupation with and passionate opposition to Japan's Security Council bid could be explained by its concerns about state security, one would expect to see a number of different outcomes. To begin with, if one were to take into account the consideration that China was simply concerned about the erosion of its power were the veto to be extended to other member states of the United Nations, *it should then, in principle, be opposed to the entire concept of the enlargement of the Security Council*. But in fact, China is not concerned about extending permanent membership in the Security Council to any of the other states besides Japan. In the case of Germany, for example, China is not only explicitly supportive of its candidacy but even holds it up as an example for Japan.

China points out that Germany has sincerely apologized to its victims and made adequate gestures of contrition for its past, and it thus deserves a seat on the UN Security Council. On 5 April, China declared that Japan's support for the Iraq War showed that it still retained the militaristic spirit of the past while Germany, another aggressor during World War II, had explicitly expressed its concern about the war. An article in *People's Daily* went on to state that Japan's facing up to its history was a necessary precondition of Chinese support for Japanese permanent membership.[30] Another article on 15 April, declared that while Germany had repented for its crimes, Japan had taken the opposite route.[31] When the Chinese Ministry of Foreign Affairs spokesperson Qin Gang was asked about China's position on Germany's bid for the Security Council, he stated that China supported Germany's playing a greater role in the United Nations.[32]

One may also argue that the issue is not the enlargement of the Security Council per se but rather the fact that Japan poses a potential threat to China that leads China to oppose Japan's bid but not Germany's. But this argument too is negated by the fact that China supports India's bid for a permanent seat—despite India's status as a nuclear weapons state on China's border with whom China has clashed in war and with whom it shares, to this day, a sensitive and unresolved conflict over territory. *Security concerns would dictate that China should oppose vehemently India's entry into the council.* Yet, at a press conference in India during the April riots, when Prime Minister Wen Jiabao was asked about China's position on India's Security Council bid, he replied that because India with its huge population was an important developing country, it had an important role to play in international society, and China completely understood and supported India's international position including its aspiration to play a greater role in the United Nations (*women gaodu zhongshi yindu zai guoji shiwu zhong fahui zhongyao zuoyong, yinwei yindu shi yige renkou zhongduo de guojia, shi yige zhongyao de fazhanzhong guojia. Women wanquan lijie he zhichi yindu zai guoji shiwu zhong, baokuo zai lianheguo fahui gengda zuoyong de yuanwang*).[33]

This is not to say that China does not feel threatened in some way by Japan. The fact that China sees itself as having been victimized by Japan and has in reality undergone the ordeal of a conquered victim is ipso facto an acknowledgment that Japan has been a threat in the past. After all, the very definition of a *victimizer* incorporates the subconscious sense of a threat. It has suffered through two major Japanese invasions involving loss of territory and subjugation and torture of its citizens. Consequently, it is averse to the emergence of a remilitarized Japan on its doorstep, but most Chinese view this as an ambiguous scenario. As Whiting points out, even the Chinese never offer probability estimates about Japan's returning to aggression. Japan is a non-nuclear and non-militarized state next to its heavily armed nuclear power neighbor, China. Whiting's extensive interviews reveal that "the future threat was left unspecified in terms of strategy, weaponry and objectives. Instead this threat was defined in general terms as being directed against China, against other Asian countries, and at times even against the United States. No one questioned this, much less explained how Japan's exceptional geographic and demographic vulnerability to nuclear retaliation would permit it to attack any one of its three nuclear neighbors."[34]

Moreover, assessments of Japan's supposedly enormous military spending are problematic. If defense spending is taken as a percentage of gross domestic product (GDP), Japan's military spending is consistently the lowest among the great powers—between 1988 and 2009, Japan's spending has never exceeded more than 1 percent of its GDP.[35] In contrast, in 2009, 2.2 percent of China's GDP, 4.4 percent of the U.S. GDP and 2.7 percent of the United Kingdom's GDP went to defense costs.[36] A reliable estimate of military expenditure (which is acknowledged as difficult to measure) should take into account more than one indicator alone. Thus, in addition, aggregates of defense spending at market exchange rates show that in 2010 Japan's military expenditure was $54,527 million—in contrast, China's was more than twice that, at $119,400 million, while the United States spent $698,281 million.[37]

Japan's large but comparatively restrained defense spending, it has been argued, makes it "unlikely to become a major military power,"[38] and ranks it "behind its major industrial competitors."[39] Moreover, during the 2004–5 period, when Sino-Japanese relations spiraled downward, there had been no "substantial increase in the threat that the [U.S.-Japan] alliance posed to the PRC . . . and while increasingly open U.S.-Japanese defense coordination with respect to the Taiwan Straits was an annoyance from the perspective of Beijing, there was little change in the actual capabilities of the two countries to intervene."[40]

China is not outraged by Japan's past because it may pose a military threat in the future, but rather it strongly believes that Japan lacks remorse for its past and has not adequately acknowledged China's suffering, and it, thus, does not deserve to be rewarded.

China's opposition to Japan's Security Council bid is not about state security. Security arguments do not provide a compelling explanation for the intensity of the 2004–5 downturn in relations, they cannot account for China's policy toward other UN Security Council aspirants, nor do they adequately reflect the limited military threat Japan actually poses to China.

Domestic Politics and War Crimes

Proponents of domestic politics explanations may claim that the ideological agenda of the Chinese government changes according to its needs. Thus its animosity toward Japan has waxed and waned according to the political climate.[41] It plays the role of a victim when it suits it. But as Yang Daqing points out, "The China-plays-history-card interpretation is not so much wrong as it sees only half the picture . . . and overestimates Beijing's role."[42] Chinese animosity toward Japan is widespread and deeply rooted in Chinese society. Students, grass roots activists, and netizens have spearheaded outbursts against Japan. The Chinese government permitted free expression on Japan in the 1980s, leading to an outpouring of anti-Japanese emotion. The Chinese government did not *create* the sentiment, rather they unleashed it. From time to time these sentiments have proved uncomfortable for the Chinese government, and they have attempted to rein them in, but, as the government is well aware, it would be a grave mistake for the regime to repress it completely or ignore public sentiment in interactions with Japan. Poor handling of the issue has the potential to create a massive backlash against the government and destabilize it. Jessica Weiss's work implicitly bolsters this argument by showing that the Chinese government allowed the 2005 anti-Japanese protests specifically to undermine Japan's bid for a permanent seat, with an end result of negotiations ultimately shifting in China's favor.[43] Given Japan's position as China's foremost trading partner, blocking Japan's bid was not risk free. If Japan had retaliated, it could have carried real economic costs for China.

Another explanation for China's implacable opposition to Japan's entry may be that it is simply a matter of war crimes and the response of a defeated nation rather than the sentiments of a victimized nation drawing on Japan's imperialist history. To begin with, in China's mind, Japan's imperialist past and World War II past are inextricably intertwined. The World War II history is seen as part and parcel of Japan's larger imperial past. The aggressions of the war are the most recent and focused in a long line of Japanese transgressions and infractions against China and are captured in the "hundred years of humiliation" (*bainian chiru*) theme taught in Chinese textbooks.

Moreover, if it was just an issue of war crimes, one might theorize that Russia, for example, would have the same reaction to Germany's bid as China does to Japan's. But as the Chinese themselves point out a little smugly, Putin expressed support for Germany gaining a seat on the UN Security Council—and according to them, only when Japan, like Germany, builds institutions that prevent the replay of past tragedies would it have the right to ask for a permanent seat.[44]

Japanese Imperialism and Its Consequences in China

The Chinese often use a particularly hostile and colorful epithet to refer to the Japanese people: *ri gui*, or Japanese devil. This short, bitter phrase encapsulates a long history of domination and real and perceived atrocities at the hands of the Japanese. Chinese animosity toward Japan stems not only from the Japanese atrocities of World War II but also from the painful consequences of the Sino-Japanese War of 1894–95.[45]

The war of 1894–95 was a domestic and international catastrophe for China. As Rose points out: "[On] the eve of the 1894 war, most Chinese felt not only condescension but also contempt for the Japanese."[46] China had considered itself the center of civilization—a state whose position of military, cultural and moral superiority had yet to be successfully challenged. Japan had been one of its vassal states in the Confucian order—the little brother to big brother China. The structure of Confucian hierarchical family relationships conferred on Japan not just duties and obligation but also a sense of inferiority vis-à-vis China. China viewed Japan as having learned from, even benefited from, superior Chinese culture and ways—Japan owed China a "cultural debt."[47] For China to be defeated then by what it considered a militarily, economically and culturally subordinate state was a huge shock. Even though China had already experienced defeat at the hands of the Western powers during the Opium Wars, defeat by Japan was in some ways even more devastating because, as Paine points out, it "forced a Chinese reappraisal of their place in the world."[48]

While the unequal treaties imposed on China by the Western powers had forced it to open its ports and concede extra-territorial rights, the defeat by Japan was the first significant loss of territory for China in modern times.[49] The Treaty of Shimonoseki in 1895 ended the war with two major consequences for China. First, the Chinese were forced to renounce the Korean peninsula. Second, and more important, the Qing had to cede Taiwan to Japan, making it a Japanese colony. China believes the Treaty of Shimonoseki decisively marked the beginning of Japanese colonialism, and humiliation and exploitation at their hands.

Japan's expansion into Chinese territory continued after the Russo-Japanese

War of 1904–5, following which Japan and Russia secretly divided nearby Chinese territory into exclusive spheres of influence. During World War I, Japan occupied Germany's holdings in Shandong province and presented China with the Twenty-One Demands for all German rights in Shandong and extra privileges in other areas. Later, 7 May 1915, the day on which Japan delivered the ultimatum that its demands be signed, became infamous in China as National Humiliation Day.[50]

The second phase of Japanese imperialism, from 1931 to 1945, began with Japan's occupation of Manchuria. The Mukden incident on 18 September 1931 marked the beginning of the Japanese takeover. The Japanese military detonated a portion of the Japanese-owned railroad near Mukden (present-day Shenyang) and then accused Chinese dissidents of orchestrating the act. This provided the Japanese Imperial Army an excuse to annex Manchuria and replace the Chinese government with a puppet state nominally headed by the last male descendant of the Qing dynasty, Puyi, at its helm. By 1937, most of the areas around Beijing had fallen under Japanese control. The Marco Polo Bridge incident, a battle between the Japanese Imperial Army and the Guomindang forces on 7 July 1937, signaled all-out war between Japan and China and is seen as the beginning of the second Sino-Japanese War. Between 1931 and 1945 the Japanese constructed an efficient informal empire in China,[51] engaging in military conquest, economic development and population settlement.[52] During this period, the Chinese assert that Japan was responsible for large-scale casualties and destruction, including the death of some 3.8 million soldiers, the killing or maiming of 18 million civilians, and the ruin of $120 billion of property.[53]

The most infamous example of Japanese imperialism, accounts of which are handed down through Chinese collective memory as well as government propaganda, is the Nanjing Massacre. From August to December 1937, the Japanese laid siege to and invaded Nanjing, the capital of China. The Japanese occupation led to mass killings, rape and looting. By some accounts, Japanese forces slaughtered 300,000 Chinese. One of the best known, sensational and controversial books on the Nanjing Massacre, *The Rape of Nanjing* by Iris Chang, vividly catalogued the horrors of the siege and brought the carnage to international attention:

> The Rape of Nanjing should be remembered not only for the number of people slaughtered but for the cruel manner in which many met their deaths. Chinese men were used for bayonet practice and in decapitation contests. An estimated 20,000–80,000 women were raped. Many soldiers went beyond rape to disembowel women, slice off their breasts, nail them alive to walls. Fathers were forced to rape their daughters, and sons their mothers, as other family members watched. Not

only did live burials, castration, the carving of organs, and the roasting of people become routine, but more diabolical tortures were practiced, such as hanging people by their tongues on iron hooks or burying people to their waists and watching them get torn apart by German shepherds. So sickening was the spectacle that even the Nazis in the city were horrified, one proclaiming the massacre to be the work of "bestial machinery."[54]

As Eykholt points out, "[F]or the Chinese, the Nanjing Massacre is an immediate symbol of outrages committed by Japanese troops during the war and of China's victimization by imperialist aggression."[55] While the Chinese accounts of the Nanjing Massacre are hotly disputed by many Japanese and some Western scholars,[56] there is no doubt that in China, Japan's conquest of Nanjing is steeped in infamy.

PII, Victimhood and Chinese Perceptions of Japanese Imperialism

The scars of Japanese imperialism run deep in China today. As Rozman points out, "[Japan's] history provides the greatest legitimacy for Chinese nationalism."[57] The "history problem" (lishi wenti) between China and Japan has periodically resulted in bursts of bitter and emotional conflict over the history of Japanese aggression during and prior to World War II.[58] For the Chinese, the issue is not simply that they suffered at the hands of the Japanese in the past. It is that they believe, first, that there is a significant discrepancy between Chinese and Japanese accounts of that history and, second, that the Japanese display a shocking lack of sensitivity to Chinese emotions and little remorse about their war crimes.

The Chinese government has at different stages emphasized different aspects of the history of the Sino-Japanese War. During Mao's time, the emphasis was on the communist victories, and the governments stressed that the atrocities of the war were the work of a handful of hard-line Japanese militarists.[59] However Whiting points out that all existing images of the Japanese were negative—"films, plays, novels, and children's picture booklets depicted the Japanese soldier as a lustful and brutal being. Japan epitomized the rapacious imperialist world that had preyed on China's weakness."[60]

When China and Japan normalized relations in 1972 China decided to forgo reparations, and in return the Japanese provided economic aid as well as an acknowledgment that they bore some responsibility for past wrongs committed against the Chinese.[61] Thus in exchange for diplomatic relations, Japan's war crimes were largely swept under the carpet. It was only during the 1980s, after

China opened up its economy (*gaige kaifang*), that the erosion of communist ideology required an infusion of legitimizing ideas to ensure public support. Patriotism, emphasizing the past greatness of China and its subsequent suffering at foreign hands, was thus encouraged. Anti-Japanese sentiments had always been present in popular narratives and collective memory. What is different in the 1980s is that they were not only allowed to flourish but also enshrined in history textbooks and heavily promoted through war memorials, conferences and films.[62]

While it is true that the Chinese government has harnessed anti-Japanese emotions for its political ends—attempting to play them up or rein them in depending on the political climate and the government's needs[63]—there is also no doubt that outrage against Japanese aggression has remained deep-rooted in Chinese society. In the 1970s, Japan's acknowledgment of the need for "self-reflection" about its war record was seen as a superficial gesture of remorse, falling short of an apology. Although there was an official ban on any academic research on the history of the war and state textbooks glossed over war atrocities, private stories of personal suffering survived and circulated within families and communities.[64] The official acknowledgment of anti-Japanese sentiment in the 1980s opened up a floodgate of emotions, and in an increasingly open society the government has been unable to stem the tide of anti-Japanese anger.

The opening of cultural space for remembering trauma continued further after 1990. Nationalism, and specifically anti-Japanese nationalism, has continued to rise in China. Bestselling books such as *China Can Say No* (*Zhongguo keyi shuo bu*), *China Can Still Say No* (*Zhongguo haishi neng shuo bu*), and *Japan: A Country That Is Unable to Admit Its Guilt* (*Riben: yige bukeng fuzui de guojia*) tapped into a deep well of Japan-bashing sentiment, characterizing the Japanese as violent and barbaric fiends without any remorse for their inhuman behavior during the war. And in the age of the Internet, in which Chinese chatrooms and web postings are often filled with anti-Japan rants, emotions spill out quickly and venomously and instantly bring together massive numbers of supporters from all over China and the diaspora abroad. Chinese voices presenting an alternative and conciliatory point of view have been few and far between, and those who have tried—such as the liberal journalist Ma Licheng with his bold article *New Thinking on Relations with Japan* (*Duiri guanxi xin siwei*) in the journal *Strategy and Management* (*Zhanlue yu guanli*) in 2002—have been denounced as traitors for being lenient toward Japan.[65]

Not only is there popular prejudice against the Japanese people (in the form of colloquial insults that cast the Japanese as "dwarfs, pirates, charlatans and crooks,"[66] an aversion to inter-marriage, and sometimes a refusal, especially by the older generation, to learn Japanese) but there is also deep anger against the Japanese government for what is seen as its deliberate failure to redress the issue adequately. The Chinese perceive the Japanese government's periodic expressions of regret as half-hearted, insincere, and inadequately apologetic.[67] A few irritants drive Chinese indignation.

First, in 1982, it was discovered that Japanese school textbooks had been revised to whitewash Japanese aggression during the war. The Chinese government accused the Japanese Ministry of Education of deliberately falsifying history by replacing the word "aggression" with "advancement."[68] The trend continued through the 1980s and 1990s with Japanese texts portraying Japan's imperial forces as "liberating" Asia from Western dominance, whitewashing the Marco Polo Bridge incident and downplaying the Nanjing Massacre and rejecting its comparison to the Holocaust.[69]

Second, visits by prominent Japanese leaders to the Yasukuni shrine have been a severe bone of contention in China. The Yasukuni shrine is a Shinto shrine commemorating the soldiers who lost their lives in the service of Imperial Japan. It enshrines, among many others, fourteen World War II–era Class A war criminals. The shrine's museum also contains a history of Japan's role in World War II that the Chinese consider revisionist. The first time it became an international issue was in 1985, when Prime Minister Nakasone Yasuhiro officially visited the shrine to pay his respects on the fortieth anniversary of the Japanese surrender. Since then visits by successive prime ministers, including Koizumi in 2006, have roused the ire of China.[70]

Third, Japan's refusal to compensate war victims such as the "comfort women" (women forced into providing sexual services for Japanese soldiers) and forced laborers has sparked grassroots campaigns in China against Japan. Chinese activists like Tong Zeng spearheaded the compensation movement and stoked the support of the general public.

While these are issues that recurrently inflame Chinese public opinion, anti-Japanese sentiment can also be provoked by random incidents that are then perceived as a national insult or betrayal. For example, in 2001, Chinese actress Zhao Wei incurred the wrath of Chinese nationalists for modeling a short dress with the Imperial Japanese flag imprinted upon it. In 2003 there was uproar over the discovery of a sex party involving hundreds of Chinese prostitutes that Japanese businessmen had organized in the Chinese city of Zhuhai. The Japanese businessmen were accused of deliberately besmirching China, while the prostitutes were accused of being traitors. Peter Hays Gries, who has tracked

TABLE 5.1. China's Opposition to Japan's Entry into the United Nations Security Council

Goal of victimhood	China's Opposition
Adopt the position of victim	Use discourse of China's suffering, Japan's lack of adequate apology and references to history, and allow popular anti-Japanese sentiment including violence
Cast an "Other" as victimizer	Cast Japan as irresponsible, unapologetic and undeserving of the honor
Justify action by using a discourse of injustice and "entitlement"	Refuse to accept reforms and cast the UN as "rewarding" Japan simply for its wealth; equate UNSC inclusion as international acknowledgement that Japan was a benevolent power and deserved parity with China

the proliferation of anti-Japanese protests in Chinese streets and cyberspace, cautions, "Chinese animosity towards Japan is unquestionably out of control," a trend that does not bode well for Sino-Japanese relations in the twenty-first century.[71]

The common thread tying together all the anti-Japanese sentiment is that China perceives itself to be a victim and to have *suffered* at Japan's hands. Moreover, in keeping with PII, the protests call for an adequate *acknowledgment* of this fact by both Japan and the international society at large.

Japan's inclusion in the Security Council as a permanent member was seen in two ways—first, as a "reward" for being a wealthy power and, second, as giving it parity with China's status as one of the Big Five. Both aspects were anathema to the Chinese. Not only did they believe that Japan did not deserve to be rewarded for mere monetary contributions to the United Nations, but rewarding it with a coveted permanent seat meant an international acknowledgment of Japan as a responsible and benevolent power. China, on the contrary, viewed Japan as completely *irresponsible* and *undeserving,* for having inflicted suffering on China without any apology. Moreover, it believed that Japan continued to wrong and insult China by denying its past of victimization, which made it unfit and dangerous for inclusion into the exclusive club of those with veto rights. Table 5.1 shows how PII resulted in China's decision to oppose Japan's entry and to allow the popular and violent expression of anti-Japanese sentiment.

China's strong sense of victimization and desire for international recognition of this fact drove it to oppose Japan's entry into the UN Security Council and to argue that Japan did not deserve such an honor. The anti-Japanese riots that broke out over the issue provided support for this stance. Moreover, the CCP government permitted the protests despite the risk that such protests could take on an anti-regime tenor and despite the obvious threat to China's lucrative economic relationship with Japan. As Weiss has pointed out, the anti-Japanese movement was ultimately advantageous to the Chinese government, in that it forced the negotiations to shift in China's favor.[72]

Methodology and Data

To assess China's stance on the Security Council issue, I first selected and searched the *China People's Daily* online newspaper (*Renmin Wang* at http://www.people.com.cn/). As the Chinese government's mouthpiece, it provides insight into the official position of China on international issues.

The *China People's Daily* was searched for relevant articles for the years 2004 and 2005[73]—the years the issue became the focus of a storm of anti-Japanese criticism in China. To locate all possible articles on the issue, the key search term used was *zhongri guanxi* (Sino-Japanese relations). The search was then narrowed by adding the phrases *changren lishi,* or "permanent member" (of the Security Council), and *riben ruchang* or "Japan's entry" (into the Security Council).

The articles were first coded and sorted for general references to imperialism and suffering,[74] as well as specific references to Japanese imperialism and past history. Once the references to imperialism had been coded, the articles were further sorted by implicit and explicit references. *Explicit references* were defined as those that linked Japan's imperial past to China's refusal to countenance Japan's bid for the Security Council seat. In other words, they made the argument that because Japan had committed wrongs in the past and refused to take responsibility for its actions, it should not be granted a permanent seat in the UN Security Council. *Implicit references* were defined as those that alluded to Japanese imperialism and the wrongs of the past in the same article that discussed Japan's bid for a Security Council seat but did not necessarily draw a direct link.

While it is important to focus analytical attention to the stance of the CCP government through its official mouthpiece, it is also worthwhile to widen the aperture to examine how Japan's bid for permanent membership was treated in the Chinese popular media more broadly. This was done by searching Sina.com.cn, the largest Chinese-language web portal and rated by Gallup as the most popular website in China. Sina.com.cn is also more likely to yield a wider range of opinions on Sino-Japanese relations, including those calling for moderation. Sina.com.cn was also searched for the years 2004 and 2005, the time period when the issue started gathering momentum, eventually leading to the 2005 riots. Again, the portal was searched using the terms *zhongri guanxi, changren lishi* and *riben ruchang*. The articles identified in this search were sorted into two broad categories: factual reports of UNSC reform and Japan's effort to secure permanent membership, and analytical articles expressing opinion or attempting to identify motives for the move. The former category was discarded, as these were simple reports of facts with no opinion. The latter category was further sorted into three types: those that did not mention history but mentioned China; those that mentioned history (implicit reference); those that mentioned history and mentioned China (explicit reference). The latter two categories stood as evidence of a mentality of victimhood on this matter.

Japan's bid to become a permanent member of the UN Security Council gained prominence in China toward the latter half of 2004. On 17 September 2004, the associate editor of *Huanqiu Shibao*, Hu Xijin, discussed Sino-Japanese relations and Japan's goal of permanent membership in an online forum and answered questions from web users. He insisted that in order for Japan to become a major political power, it needed to increase its "soft power"—that is, its "moral influence" (*zuowei yige zhengzhi daguo riben hai xuyao zuo yixie shiqing, cengjia yixie ruanshili, ye jiushi tade daode yingxiangli*).[75] His implicit meaning was clear—that Japan had not adequately squared up to its past and therefore lacked the moral caliber for China to support its bid for a seat in the Security Council. An article on 15 December was more explicit. It declared that while it had been suggested that Japan's significant contribution to the United Nations was an important reason why it should be offered a permanent seat in the Security Council, the UN was after all not a "stock company," and authority did not emerge from monetary contributions alone (*you yulun jiu shuo, riben chang ba "jiaona huifei duo, guoji gongxian da" guazai zuibian, dan lianheguo bu shi gufen gongsi, bu neng anchuqian duoshao jueding fayanquan*)—especially when Japan had a record of disrespect for international responsibility.[76]

The issue gained momentum in 2005 with various objections, all related to the perceived lack of Japanese repentance for its past war record, offered for China's opposition to Japanese permanent membership on the Security Council. An article on 27 March remonstrated that the textbook controversy was crucial for Sino-Japanese relations. If Japan could not even properly educate its youth and cultivate an honest attitude toward its history, how could it expect to further its ambitions in the Security Council?[77]

Figure 5.1 demonstrates how the issue gathered momentum from January through March and reached a crisis point in April when the anti-Japanese riots broke out. A flurry of articles and editorials were devoted to the issue in April,

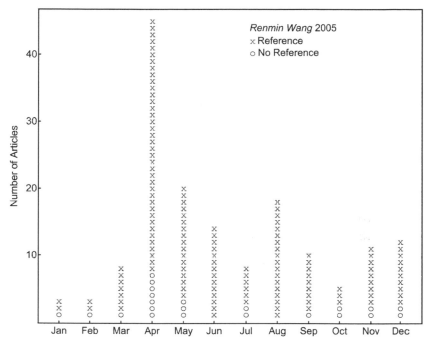

FIG. 5.1. Total References to Japanese Imperialism. Source: *Renmin Wang* 2005.

the majority of them explicitly linking Japan's quest and Japan's imperialist history. On 1 April, an article emphasized that if Japan does not apologize for its history of aggression, it has no right to be a member of the UN Security Council (*riben ruguo bu dui qinlue lishi daoqian de hua . . . mei zige chengwei anlihui changren lishiguo*).[78] A web posting on the same day noted that China should oppose Japanese permanent membership because it is not in China's national interest to support a country that has not yet apologized for its imperialist history and whose past means that it could pose a catastrophe for international peace (*gei shijie heping dailai zhongda zainan*).[79]

With the rising tide of anti-Japanese public opinion, the articles—both explicitly and implicitly—began commenting on the Chinese government's response to the crisis. On 5 April, Foreign Ministry spokesperson Qin Gang answered questions from the press. A reporter asked about the vandalism and damage to Japanese property in the protests. While Qin avoided making a direct statement on Japan's bid, he stated that the events revealed the dissatisfaction of the Chinese people about Japan's attitude toward China and that the Chinese government hoped that Japan would properly treat the sensitive problems, such as the interpretation of history, that affect the feelings of the Chinese people

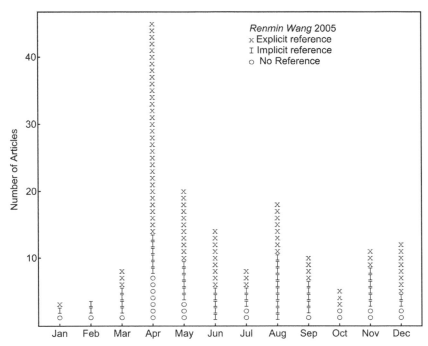

FIG. 5.2. Explicit and Implicit References to Japanese Imperialism. Source: *Renmin Wang* 2005.

(*women xiwang rifang rhenzhen duidai zhongguo renmin de guanqie, tuoshan chuli lishi deng sheji zhongguo renmin ganqing minggan wenti*).[80] An article on 7 April discussed the growing movement in Chinese cities and online to collect signatures against Japanese permanent membership and stated that although the Chinese government had cautioned against unrestrained protest, it could not ignore public opinion, which was overwhelmingly against the move (*zhongguo zhengfu bu keneng hushi minyi de cunzai. Cong wangluo pinglun dao xianshi zhongde jietou qianming, zhongguoren dui riben chengwei anlihui changren lishiguo fachu de jihu quan shi fandui zhisheng*).[81]

Although the riots were sparked by Chinese opposition to Japanese permanent membership, other emotional issues tied intricately to Japan's past history emerged in public outbursts. On 11 April, a web posting, referring to the issue of comfort women, passionately declared that just as someone with a record of sexual crimes cannot be a responsible person, so a country with 200,000 Chinese comfort women on its record of sexual abuse absolutely cannot become a responsible member of the UN Security Council (*daizhe yige xingfan-zui jilu de ren buhui shi yige you zerengan de ren, daizhe 20 wan "zhongguo weianfu" xingqiangbao he xingnuedai jilu de, ye juedui de buneng chengwei dui guoji he shijie you zerengan de anlihui chengyuan).*[82] On 14 April, Chinese official Tang Jiaxuan spoke about the impasse and was quoted as saying that the visits to the Yasukuni shrine were an inevitable problem in Sino-Japanese relations, and China would certainly not change its position toward its interpretation of history.[83]

In late April, the meeting between Hu and Koizumi failed to resolve the issue, and an article on the meeting commented that to be a member of the UN Security Council is to be "responsible," and till that point, Japan had not given the impression of being a "responsible" country (*riben zhijin weineng chenggong de shuliqi "fu zeren" de xingxiang*).[84]

The riots simmered down by the end of April, but the issue remained in the Chinese consciousness through the rest of the year. The entire gamut of grievances in Sino-Japanese relations were referenced as obstacles to Japanese permanent membership. An article stated that in order for Japan to gain a more influential position in the world (an implicit reference to the Security Council), it needed to alter its textbooks, cease visits to the Yasukuni shrine, and respect history and reality.[85] On 3 June, an article began with a strong statement: "History is a mirror and the interpretation of the past reflects the attitude and judgment of the people of the present. . . . While history examines the past and helps people make the right choices in the future, it also exposes the ugly performances which attempt to distort the truth" (*lishi shi yimian jingzi, tongguo dui guowang shijian de pingjia zheshe shechu jintian renmen dui shi yufei, zhengyi yu xie'e de butong jiazhi panduan. Lishi zai jingjian guoqu gei weilai tigong zhengque xuanze de tongshi, ye biran dongchuan naxie waiqu lishi de chou'e biaoyan).*[86] A few days later, visits to the Yasukuni shrine were deemed unacceptable because it worshipped criminals whose hands were tainted with the blood of the peoples of victimized nations (*jingguo shensheli gongfengzhe bei yuandong guoji junshifating shenpan de jiaji zhanfan. Zhexie zhanfan shi riben junguozhuyi de yuanxiong. Tamen de shuangshou zhanman le shouhaiguo renmin de xianxue).*[87]

The approaching sixtieth anniversary of the Sino-Japanese War in August contributed to another spike in anti-Japanese articles protesting Japan's bid. On 3 August an editorial declared that soon it would be the anniversary of the Sino-Japanese War, and one would expect Japan to be deeply repentant toward China and the world; yet the country was less repentant than ever (*zai zhongguo kangri zhanzheng yu shijie fan faxisi zhanzheng shengli 60 zhounian zhiji, anzhao changli, riben yinggai shi dizitai xiang zhongguo he shijie biaoda qi chanhui he fansi de, danshi jieran xiangfan riben jinnian gaodiao de fanchang).*[88] Another stated that if Japan wanted political status on par with its economic status in the world, it needed to face the history of sixty years ago honestly, admit its war crimes, be responsible, apologize to China and the other victimized countries and obtain their forgiveness (*riben ru yao genshang yazhou ji shijie dachao, chengdan yuqi jingji diwei xiangchen de guoji zeren, yu yazhou geguo gongcun gongrong, shouxian jiu yao chengshi zhengque de duidai 60 nian qian na duan lishi, zhimian zhanzheng zuize, fuqi lishi zeren, xiang zhongguo yazhou ge shouhaiguo zhencheng daoqian, zhengqu zhongguo ji yazhou ge shouhaiguo de liangjie*).[89]

Interestingly and probably unsurprisingly (given past high-profile incidents with Ma Licheng and Zhao Wei), there are exceedingly few dissenting Chinese voices expressing support for Japan or playing down the significance of Japanese permanent membership. Some of the alternative views that did exist attempted to bolster Chinese confidence rather than remonstrate the violence of anti-Japan sentiments. On 4 August, for example, a web posting argued that there was no need to protest against the textbook issue or visits to Yasukuni, and China should learn from the example of the United States, which does not protest against the Japanese textbook descriptions of Pearl Harbor because it is a real great power and brushes off such outright lies.[90] A few articles point out the benefits of a good relationship with Japan. A chapter from a book by Lu Gang and Guo Xueteng called *Interpreting the China Threat* (*Zhongguo weixie shei? Jiedu zhongguo weixielun*),[91] published in *Renmin Ribao*,[92] pointed out Japan's contribution in aiding China during the SARS crisis and other "laudable behavior" and advised that the history problem be solved. It did, however, qualify that "even so, some principles cannot be compromised, the history problem being one. If we [the Chinese] don't have the courage to express anger against the worship of war criminals then we lose our right to be humans and the dignity of our people will vanish to nothing" (*raner youxie yuanze shi buneng biandong de, lishi wenti juebuneng hanhu. Yinwei womende fuzhi shi yao kao xianbeimen zaitianzhiling baoyoude, dang women zhexie houbei lian dui gongfeng zhanzheng zuifan de xingwei biaoshi fennu de yongqi dou meiyou le, women ye jiu sangshi le zuoren de zige, women minzu de zunyan ye jiang zai xianshizhuyi de mihuntang zhong huaweiwuyou*).[93]

It is very clear from the survey of *Renmin wang* in 2005 that the goal of victimhood is strongly intertwined with China's position on Japanese permanent membership on the Security Council. As Figure 5.2 shows, a full 86 percent of the articles contained either implicit or explicit references to Japanese imperialism and China's past history of suffering. It is a measure of how sensitive the issue is that although the government has in the past reined in anti-Japanese sentiment, including after the April riots, its official mouthpiece continued to carry articles on the topic, the majority of which focused on Japan's history of aggression.

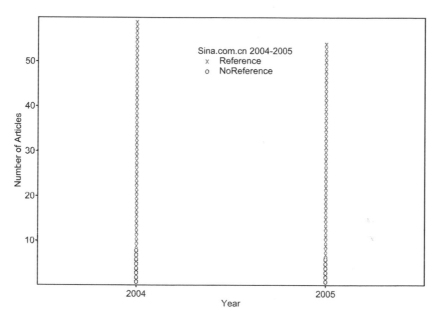

FIG. 5.3. Total References to Japanese Imperialism. Source: Sina.com.cn, 2004 and 2005.

This is given further weight when Sina.com.cn is searched. Figure 5.3 shows that in 2004, 86 percent of the articles linked the history issue to Japan's quest for a Security Council seat. In 2005, this increased to 89 percent.

Even in 2004, when the issue was just emerging, articles on Sina.com. cn reflected the outrage that would eventually emerge in the April riots. An article from *Zhongguo Xinwen Wang* on 22 September baldly asked, "Without deep introspection about history, how can Japan enter the Security Council?" (*bu shenke fanxing lishi ri ruhe jin anlihui*).[94] In addition to reports, both those explicitly citing Japan's lack of apology for its past as well as those referencing Japan's history problem without mentioning China, ample coverage was given to the "views" of countries that opposed Japan's bid on the basis of history. A few examples:

South Korea [says that] to obtain a permanent seat Japan should first change its attitude towards Asia (*hanguo: riben huo changrenxi bixu xian gaibian dui yazhou taidu*);[95] Japan should first be clear about the crimes of its history of aggression: North Korea challenges Japan's scheme to get a permanent seat (*ying xian qingsuan zuie de quinlueshi chaoxian zhiyi riben mou "chang"*).[96]

Awkwardly for Japan, none of its neighboring countries applaud its UNSC bid (*yu huo anlihui changren lishiguo xiwei linguo wu hecai riben gangga*).[97]

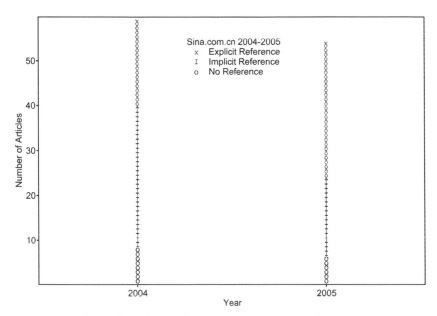

FIG. 5.4. Explicit and Implicit References to Japanese Imperialism. Source: Sina.com. cn, 2004 and 2005.

The survey of *Renmin wang* and Sina.com.cn shows that, whether discussed in the official media or in the mainstream media, the majority of articles link Japan's attempt to secure a permanent seat on the UN Security Council to Japan's "history problem." Some do so by explicitly stating that Japan needs to apologize before it can be rewarded with a seat; others imply that morality is a criterion for increasing influence, or highlight the ire of neighboring countries that support China's opposition.

While it is true that the Chinese government probably knew about the 2005 protests in advance, and eventually moved to rein in the anti-Japanese activists,[98] the official and popular positions on Japan's bid matched. There was deep antipathy to the idea of Japan, a country guilty of victimizing China and unrepentant of its past, occupying a permanent seat in the UN Security Council. Whether one agrees with Weiss that the government deliberately and successfully utilized this popular anti-Japanese sentiment to bolster its own opposition (in August 2005, China and the United States jointly agreed to oppose the addition of permanent members),[99] or if one speculates that the mass anti-Japanese hysteria simply went amok, eventually leading the government to clamp down, the point remains that, first, the popular opposition stemmed from a sense of victimhood and grievance about Japan's unapologetic history, and, second, that the government allowed these protests, with a concomitant risk of backlash and an even more considerable risk of harming Sino-Japanese economic ties, until the Japanese bid stalled. Thus the dominant goal of PII to be recognized as a victim drove China's decision to oppose Japan's entry into the UN Security Council.

Conclusion

The dominant goal of the victimhood is the most important component of PII. This chapter has shown that the goal of victimhood can be used to analyze an important foreign policy choice made by China: to oppose Japan's entry into the UN Security Council as a permanent member in 2004–5. It is clear from *Renmin wang* and Sina.com.cn that, overwhelmingly, articles dealing with the issue of Japan's permanent membership also made either an explicit or an implicit link to Japan's past history, China's suffering and Japan's lack of remorse and apology. Despite Japan's position as China's foremost trading partner and the inevitable impact on bilateral trade, China not only publicly opposed Japan's entry into the UN Security Council but also sanctioned violent and widespread anti-Japanese demonstrations in the country.

While one could conceivably claim that a sense of victimization should only exist among formerly colonized states immediately after decolonization, as the cases of India's nuclear decision in 1998 and China's opposition to Japan in the UN Security Council show, it is startling that the trauma of colonialism influences foreign policy more than half a century after decolonization.

Conclusion

In 2005, Prime Minister Manmohan Singh gave a speech at Oxford University in which he paid tribute to the "beneficial consequences" of British rule in India, including respect for the rule of law, modern universities, a strong civil service, and principles of constitutional government. Back home, the Indian press and politicians, particularly those from the opposition Bharatiya Janata Party, seized upon his statements and lambasted him for "humiliating Indian freedom fighters" and "bowing before foreign rule."[1]

In 2008, hundreds of Chinese demonstrated against Carrefour, a French supermarket chain, after Nicholas Sarkozy, then president of France, threatened to boycott the opening ceremony of the Beijing Olympic Games.[2] A large placard declared, "Say no to Carrefour!!! Say no to French Imperialists!!! Strongly protest the Anglo-French invasion of China in 1860; Strongly protest the slander of Beijing Olympics in 2008; Strongly protest France's interference of [sic] China's internal affairs; Strongly protest the French media's distortion of facts; Strongly protest Carrefour's financial support to Dalai Lama. Chinese? Stand up!!!"[3]

These two anecdotes are vivid demonstrations of a mentality of victimhood that persists in India and China. These countries *defeated* colonialism over six decades ago. Yet the sense of victimization in these countries is pervasive, leading to constant invocations of their colonial past. What do I mean by a mentality of victimhood in these countries? It is a conviction that they are the victims and other countries are victimizers. A sense that they have suffered and that consequently, this suffering needs to be acknowledged by international society. A sense that *because* they have suffered they are *entitled* to sympathy, understanding and even concessions. There are many such incidents that reflect how wide-spread the consciousness of suffering and humiliation is.

An Indian political commentator, Ashok Malik, told me the Indian media often subscribes to a "why do they hate us?" mentality. He recalled a 2008 television roundtable in which he was a participant. An Indian student had been assaulted in Australia. Malik remembered the anchor opening: "[F]irst Idi Amin's Uganda, then the dot busters in America, now Indian students being beaten in Australia. Why do they hate us?" He said the other guest on the show, an Indian diplomat, responded by "talking about white Australia policy and Bob Hawke's Australia—at which point, the anchor nodded sagely." Malik said ruefully he realized then that any reasonable analysis he put forth was going to be met with more examples, no matter how old, of supposedly ubiquitous anti-Indian sentiment abroad, particularly in the West.[4]

This mentality of victimhood can be seen too in China today. Take China's role in the recent Olympics. While, as the *Economist* observed, "the sense of victimhood is not confined to the Olympics,"[5] these sentiments were often conspicuous during the games because the accolades and medals won by the Chinese were portrayed domestically as "unassailable evidence that China has finally 'made it.'"[6] During the Olympics, when Ye Shiwen faced suspicions of performance enhancing drug use, the conservative Chinese *Global Times* stated, "[N]egative comments about (Ye) and Chinese athletes come from deep bias and reluctance from the Western press to see Chinese people make break-throughs."[7] A headline in the *People's Daily* declared, "At the Olympics the arrogance and prejudice of the West towards China can be seen."[8]

At these same Olympics, the *Global Times* explained China's preoccupation with its gold medal tally as "historical." "China was known as the sick man of Asia, torn by war and poverty. . . . It is understandable that China puts weight on gold medals."[9] As Wang points out, "[T]he Sick Man of East Asia" is a "special national discourse . . . [that] has long been regarded by many Chinese as a humiliating epithet used by Western imperialists to refer both to the poor physical health of the Chinese people and to China itself. . . . [It] has loomed in the Chinese imagination as an insulting label applied to China by Japan and the West."[10]

But even beyond open demonstrations of victimhood sentiment, whether at the Olympics, or during the accidental bombing of the Chinese embassy in Belgrade in 1999, or the EP-3 incident in 2001, China often claims solidarity with other nations that have "suffered." During a visit to South Africa in 2007, Chinese president Hu Jintao went to great pains to reject any notion that

China was behaving like a colonial power in Africa.[11] He declared that China too wanted to stand up to "rich bullies" and that the "colonial aggressions and oppression by foreign powers" in China meant that they would never behave in the same fashion.[12]

More than six decades have passed since the British left India. Yet British colonialism remains a sensitive and often toxic issue in India. China's brush with colonialism was very different from India's experience. India was ruled by the British for nearly two hundred years. China experienced piecemeal colonialism, leading Mao to dub it a "semi-colony." Yet the Chinese go to great pains, even today, to emphasize their colonial history and even more, significantly their victimization by colonial powers. These constant references to an increasingly distant time period, a period that indeed concluded with the defeat of colonial forces by these societies, are quite remarkable.

How do these feelings of humiliation and emphasis on victimization and suffering translate into concrete foreign policy behavior? The mentality of victimhood and consciousness of suffering are the sources of post-imperial ideology, or PII. PII has three goals—the dominant goal of victimhood driving the subordinate goals of maximizing territorial sovereignty and maximizing status.

PII manifests itself in recurrent political behaviors. These countries, first, adopt the position of victim and cast the other state in the role of victimizer. Second, they justify their behavior and negotiating posture by appeals against oppression and discrimination. Third, they adhere to strict concepts of the inviolability of borders. Fourth, they exhibit marked sensitivity to any loss of face in international interactions and can be obsessive in their efforts to "regain" lost status. PII has the greatest explanatory value when sovereignty is threatened, non-negotiable borders are at stake, or prestige is on the line. As the empirical chapters have documented, the behavior of India and China is not fully understandable in the absence of an historical understanding of how PII serves as an enduring reaction to the trauma of colonialism. India and China are not merely rising powers, they are rising powers whose actions flow from specific historical circumstances.

Therefore, two extremely important questions underpin this book. First, how should the study of international politics treat colonialism? Colonialism is a phenomenon that, since decolonization, has received ample attention across several academic disciplines. Academics from literature, history, anthropology, sociology and, to some extent, political science have debated and acknowledged the significance of colonialism. In popular discussions, it plays a recurrent role in analyses of conflict and development—in 2010, for example, Nicholas Kristof, the prominent *New York Times* columnist, touched on the question of whether all of Africa's problems could be laid at the door of colonialism.[13]

Given the impact of colonialism, the many discussions of it in academic and non-academic circles is unsurprising. Colonialism affected a vast swath of countries. Colonial choices and the often hasty process of decolonization created territorial conflicts that persist. Apart from its sheer reach, the word itself, "colonialism," carries powerful connotations about military, economic and cultural dominance. To this day, subjugation, hierarchy, power grabbing, racism, exploitation, inequity, injustice and violence are some of the concepts that are associated with it. As Dirks points out, "[C]olonialism was made possible, and then sustained and strengthened, as much by cultural technologies of rule as it was by the more obvious and brutal modes of conquest that first established power on foreign shores."[14]

Yet despite the varied discussions of it, there has been little systematic treatment of colonialism as an independent variable in international relations. How should one systematically analyze the phenomenon of colonialism? Its history clearly matters to the countries that experienced it. This book acknowledges the weight of their colonial past and moves to understand its causal power through the lens of trauma theory. In doing so, it offers a path to understanding *why and how* colonialism still matters to these countries.

Having shown in Chapter 1 that the experience of colonialism can be understood as trauma, Chapter 2 used statistical analysis to establish the existence of a discourse of victimhood in former colonized states. Using a new method to analyze speeches from 1993 to 2007 in the United Nations, it shows, with statistical significance, that there is a difference in discourse between states that have been colonized and those that have not. That difference arises from a strong sense of victimhood.

Thus the second and narrower question that has underpinned this book is, how does such a transformative historical event affect the behavior of the large number of actors in international society that were subject to extractive colonialism? Specifically, how should we understand countries like India and China, which despite very different colonial experiences, call—even demand—attention to their past?

Even today, decades after its demise, colonialism is a significant event that influences their foreign policy decisions because it is perceived and responded to as trauma. Thus these countries have a dominant goal of victimhood. This means that they seek recognition and empathy for their role as a victim in the international system. The goal of victimhood has a corresponding sense of entitlement, and this manifests itself in two subordinate goals—maximizing territorial sovereignty and maximizing status. Together, I have termed these three goals post-imperial ideology, or PII, and shown that it influences their international behavior.

India and China make excellent cases. They differ on many political, economic and social factors. Also, they experienced vastly different manifestations of colonialism. Yet they have a similar response to their past in the form of PII. I have demonstrated that the commonality they share is their regard for the humiliations of colonialism as trauma, and that this trauma directly led to PII. The fact that PII emerged in both cases despite these differences presents a strong test for my argument about the transformative effect of colonialism and its impact on subsequent international behavior. Second, India and China are excellent cases because they are rising powers and their behavior is substantively important to contemporary global politics. PII provides a lens through which their behavior can be understood, furnishing explanations for that behavior rather than merely positing security goals or revisionist intentions. India and China persistently claim that their past is important, and this book has analyzed why and how that is the case. Third, India and China are intriguing cases that demand even more attention beyond this book's initial analyses. It is reasonable to speculate that India's and China's status as rising powers and as holders of post-imperial ideology interacts in ways that make them emphasize their past even more than other formerly colonized states. As they define themselves in a new international order, narratives about their past may be a particularly compelling way to present their identity and create an international understanding of who they are.

This book has argued that colonialism generated narratives of injustice and exploitation. Do India and China display an objective portrayal of history and events as they actually took place? Almost certainly not. Both Indian and Chinese government accounts of colonial history have, as I have mentioned earlier in this text, been disputed. Moreover, China has an authoritarian regime while India is a democracy. This suggests that the Chinese government should have, to put it bluntly, greater control over its message. But as Japan's case shows, that is not necessarily the case. The commonality in narratives suggests that the common transformative episode of colonialism is at work, rather than mere regime manipulation of messages.

The image of India or China as victims of colonialism resonates with the public and ties into nationalist emotions. The references to past suffering cannot be dismissed as mere government propaganda. Their colonial past is seen as trauma and responded to as trauma. This leads both states to frame their issues in terms of victim and victimizer in the international arena. The victimizer may or may not be one who has aggressed against the former colonized state in the past. Contemporary victimizers may merely evoke similar responses, despite having no responsibility for past transgressions. Post-colonial states are hypersensitive to any possible hint of coercion or insult, of discrimination or exclusion.

PII, therefore, explains behavior on important foreign policy issues where such countries feel that their sovereignty is threatened, that borders they consider non-negotiable are at stake, or feel they will suffer a loss of face or decline in prestige. Chapters 3, 4 and 5 discussed specific foreign policy decisions of India and China and use PII as an independent variable to explain them.

Chapter 3 examined the failure of the 1960 border negotiations between India and China. These were the last negotiations between the two countries before they went to war in 1962. It traced how the interaction of the three goals of PII led to the failure of negotiations and, consequently, a border war that still affects relations between the two countries. It also showed that PII existed in these two countries in the years immediately after decolonization.

Chapter 4 moved forward to the contemporary period to show that PII and, specifically, victimhood matter today. It analyzed India's decision to declare nuclear weapons state status in 1998. Using PII, it explained why India decided to conduct further nuclear tests twenty-four years after the first round of tests in 1974. To do so, it utilized articles in the Indian print media in 1974 and in the 1990s to show that a sense of victimization and entitlement in association with the nuclear issue absent in 1974 had appeared by the time of the 1998 decision.

Chapter 5 continued in the contemporary period and focused on Sino-Japanese relations, which matter hugely for stability in Asia as well as Japan's alliance with the United States. It focused on China's decision to oppose Japan's entry into the UN Security Council as a permanent member in 2005, a position China continues to hold. Using articles in the Chinese print and electronic media, it demonstrated that the dominant goal of victimhood explains China's hostility to the idea of Japan as a permanent member of the Security Council.

The analysis of colonialism and the PII framework explored by this book makes three important contributions to existing understandings of international relations. First, it systematically treats history, specifically colonialism, as an explanatory variable. By examining trauma theory and showing how colonialism is treated as collective historical trauma by the countries that have experienced it, it offers an understanding of why the narrative of suffering and victimhood is important to countries like India and China, and why it affects how they see the international system.

Second, it offers a new way to analyze two crucial states, India and China. As rising powers, the dominant explanation for their behavior has been the pursuit of security. This book, instead, argues that India's and China's repeated affirmations of the importance of their past should not be disregarded. More so, it finds that their foreign policy behavior is only interpretable in light of that past, and is not sufficiently explained by traditional security-seeking explanations. Failure to acknowledge the importance of these twin variables—colonialism leading to PII—could result in policy errors. India's and China's emphasis of their colonial past means that the sense of victimhood and its corollary, a sense of entitlement to recover that which was lost, needs to be an important component of any discourse of "engaging" or "managing" these two powers.

Analysts have struggled to agree on India's nuclear restraint in 1974 and cannot adequately explain why India decided to conduct nuclear tests in 1998. The nuclear tests may indeed have had the effect of enhancing India's security, but without an understanding that India had a strong grievance against a discriminatory and exclusionary nuclear system, one cannot put forward an explanation of its decision to test in 1998. By 1998, India's security environment was generally safer than it had been for decades. What changed is how discriminatory India viewed the international nonproliferation system to be. Similarly, I show that an analysis of China's and Japan's relationship, a relationship that is vital to stability in Asia and a constitutive element of the U.S.-China-Japan triangle, is incomplete unless one understands China's preoccupation with past victimization at the hands of Japan.

Third, PII is generalizable. It offers a way to categorize states and ensures that the international behavior of a wide range of states with differing regimes and power structures can be analyzed. Theories of offensive and defensive realism and predictions of state behavior such as balancing, bandwagoning or bargaining refer primarily to states with material capabilities significant enough to matter. As weaker states, developing nations are mostly ignored. This book has focused on India and China. While today their material capabilities are sufficient for them to matter in structural accounts of international relations, that was not always the case. Despite this, they charted policies that were often contrary to the structural incentives of the international system, policies that had meaningful effects on international politics. This project develops an analytic apparatus that places developing nations with a history of colonialism at its center, rather than relegating them to the periphery.

Norm-based theories, too, have a two-pronged gap. First, their primary focus is on states with the ability to impose or break norms—obviously, norms held by states that are perceived as "successful" (usually Western states) are more likely to be adopted.[15] This focus on developed states is even apparent when examining the problems of developing nations. For example, when answering the important question of why Asia never developed a large mutual defense treaty like NATO, Hemmer and Katzenstein point to the "importance of a sense of identity in forming alliances."[16] They argue that the United States identified with Europe primarily because of "an undeniable racial component. . . . Even as colonialism was ending the colonial mindset remained strong." Therefore, the United States did not push for a NATO in Asia. Despite the correct acknowledgment of identity in shaping behavior in the security arena, their answer centers on the United States and fails to reference the response and attitude of Asian nations. While U.S. foreign policy at the time may have been dominated by men such as Dulles who distinguished between strong, white Europe and weak, non-white, inferior Asia, Asian foreign policy was dominated by men who were *acutely aware* that such distinctions were being made in the West. Jawaharlal Nehru, for instance, could barely abide Dulles.[17] It is entirely conceivable that there was no NATO in Asia also because many Asian nations had a strong anti-colonial stance, the United States was often cast as an imperialist power and they were extremely sensitive to any hints of racism.

Second, even when developing countries do receive attention, the shared experience of colonialism is very rarely seen as a method of categorizing them. Rather, they are mostly distinguished from developed nations either on the basis of disparities in economic structures and material capabilities,[18] or in terms of the external and internal problems they face.[19] Sometimes this is taken a slight step further to include state-society relations and political culture.[20]

But colonialism, while referred to casually and continually, is not used systematically as a tool to categorize states or analyze behavior. When mentioned, it is pointed to as a general experience out of which may arise somewhat vague yet stark ideas about the world—West/non-West division, Western brutality, neo-colonialism, "insulting" imperial borders.[21] This kind of theorizing fails to recognize that while these ideas may loosely exist, they cross geographical divisions in foreign policy. Rather than a black-and-white vision of the world divided into the West and the rest (a vision perhaps more prevalent during the actual period of decolonization), India and China, for example, have a more nuanced conception of themselves and the countries with which they are dealing. Thus, India and China each see the other as the victimizer in the Sino-

Indian border conflict, and China *rejects* imperial borders while India *accepts* them.

Some norm scholars have come very close to acknowledging the importance of colonial history in foreign policy. Acharya, for example, strongly criticizes the lack of focus on "ideational forces within the (Asian) region" when discussing security arrangements in Asia.[22] He theorizes that Asian leaders, particularly those who had been involved in the anti-colonial struggle, held strong ideas about non-intervention and the threat posed by dominant powers.[23] Clapham points out that post-colonial states have "emerged as the most strident defenders of Westphalian sovereignty in the international order."[24] However, their work is implicit rather than explicit about the importance of colonialism and does not actually utilize the colonial experience as either an independent variable or a tool to distinguish this category of states. This book has demonstrated that a large category of states—states that have experienced imperialism and colonialism—do not necessarily behave in the way that realists or liberals would necessarily predict that they would, because their common transformative historical event contributes to a powerful ideology of victimhood that dominates their decision calculus. It has argued that this categorization, and associated traits found in category members, may be better able to explain key features of foreign policy than traditional labels, such as developed versus developing states, major versus minor powers, revisionist versus status quo states, used in international relations.

This book has explored India and China as arresting examples of countries that have different experiences of colonialism but retain a similar emphasis on victimhood in international society. More broadly, it has demonstrated that the discourse of victimization is evident in countries that have experienced colonialism, as opposed to those that did not. It can be shown with statistical significance that there is a difference in the way colonized and non-colonized states use words, and this difference can be attributed to a sense of victimization. Colonized countries say they care very much about their colonial past. Drawing on this simple fact and the concept of PII, I offer up further avenues for research.

First, in the case of India and China, I have used PII to analyze several important foreign policy issues. But there are also other possible cases that offer scope for the further use of PII. The conflict over Kashmir is one of the most challenging foreign policy issues facing India today. The Kashmir dispute was born at the cusp of British decolonization in India. In 1947, the two newly independent countries of India and Pakistan went to war over the former princely state. Both countries believed this territory was integral to the national identity that the Congress Party and the Muslim League had articulated during their fight against British colonialism. Kashmir was integral to India's vision of secular nationalism and Pakistan's quest for religious nationalism.

India fervently believes (and teaches through government-issued school textbooks) that the rise of religious nationalism and the carving out of Pakistan can be attributed to deliberate British colonial policies of "divide and rule" designed to weaken the Indians and keep them subjugated. Kashmir is intricately bound up with this narrative. No Indian government can afford to preside over the loss of Kashmir. Future work should consider India's stance on Kashmir and the breakdown of the many rounds of negotiations with Pakistan through the lens of PII, particularly the interaction of the goals of victimhood and maximizing territorial sovereignty.

For China too, other cases might merit an explanation through a PII framework. Taiwan, for example, for all practical purposes a fully functioning democratic country with a developed economy, is crucial to Chinese national identity and "combines all of the worst lessons of the [colonial] century of humiliation for China."[25] Triggering strong connotations of victimization, Taiwan was first lost when the Japanese defeated Qing China and perceived as lost yet again during the Korean War, when Truman dispatched the Seventh Fleet to the Taiwan Straits, ending the possibility of a Communist takeover. Taiwan's emotional salience for China is routinely evident in Chinese behavior. It is at least plausible that events such as the 1995–96 Taiwan Straits crisis, triggered by the mere granting of a private U.S. visa to Taiwanese president Lee Teng-hui to visit his alma mater, Cornell University, might be better analyzed through a prism of victimhood.

A second avenue of research is to focus on the emergence of PII, rather than its effects. This book has used trauma theory to explain why colonialism was a transformative historical event. It established that PII exists and that a sense of victimization exists across formerly colonized states, and then turned to using PII as an independent variable to analyze the foreign policies of India and China. This leaves open the interesting sociological research question of how PII can be treated as a dependent variable. If colonialism is remembered as trauma and a sense of victimization was created, what are the exact pathways by which this is transmitted in these societies? This book has outlined what some of these pathways could be—personal stories, anecdotes, government-issued school history textbooks, international speeches, and party manifestos. This offers the rich possibility of categorizing different pathways of remembrance and collecting data on each one to create a more complete picture of how the goal of victimhood is kept relevant to the national psyche and collective memory.

Third, the detailed exploration of the pathways by which PII is transmitted and kept alive would also help answer another very important question—when does trauma go away? How long do memories of traumatic historical events last in affected societies? When do victims of colonialism realize that they are also the vanquishers of colonialism and stop feeling victimized? This is a difficult question to answer. It has been more than six decades since the demise of colonialism, and memories seem to be fresh still. Will they last another half-century or more? Perhaps concerted efforts on the part of governments, non-governmental organizations, and civil society will keep memories alive. Historical memories can be institutionalized and persist as long as the institutions last and do not change their original purpose (witness remembrances of the Holocaust, for example, are a conscious effort to create enduring memories). Certain countries may emphasize memory more than others. Some may attempt to forget. Rising powers such as India and China are interesting test cases for a future politics of memory. Their position in the international system, bumping against incumbent stakeholders, might aggravate concerns over discrimination and prestige. Their increasing military and economic capabilities give them more incentives to project a certain image of themselves internationally. All of these factors mean that the politics of victimhood may be contested and dynamic in India and China in the coming years. It will be interesting to revisit the concept of PII and victimhood in two decades to see if and how post-colonial countries, particularly India and China, still remember. But for now, PII offers a useful tool to analyze their present international behavior by drawing on their colonial past, a past that they insist is crucial to them.

Notes

Notes

Introduction

1. This book is concerned with extractive rather than settler colonialism. See Chapter 1 for more details.

2. Robert Jackson, "The Weight of Ideas in Decolonization," in *Ideas and Foreign Policy: Beliefs, Institutions, and Political Change*, ed. J. Goldstein and R. Keohane (Ithaca, NY: Cornell University Press, 1993).

3. Robert Jackson, *Quasi-States: Sovereignty, International Relations, and the Third World* (New York: Cambridge University Press, 1990), 85.

4. Jackson, "The Weight of Ideas in Decolonization," 114.

5. This is particularly evident in the works of anti-imperialist and dependency theorists, such Immanuel Wallerstein, Andre Gunder Frank and Vladimir Lenin.

6. For a discussion of norm emergence and transmission, see Martha Finnemore and Kathryn Sikkink, "International Norm Dynamics and Political Change," *International Organization* 52, no. 4 (1998): 887–917.

7. Mohammed Ayoob, "The Third World in the System of States: Acute Schizophrenia or Growing Pains?" *International Studies Quarterly* 33, no. 1 (March 1989), 68.

8. Lakshmi Iyer, "The Economic Rise of India," lecture, Boston University, 16 November 2011.

9. Vipin Narang and Paul Staniland, "Democracy's Demand?: Salience, Structure and Security Policy with Evidence from India," paper presented at CASI India Security Workshop, University of Pennsylvania, 13 April 2012.

10. Conference discussion, CASI India Security Workshop, University of Pennsylvania, 13 April 2012.

11. Suisheng Zhao, "China's Pragmatic Nationalism: Is It Manageable?," *Washington Quarterly* 29, no. 1 (2005); Jessica Weiss, "Powerful Patriots: Nationalism, Diplomacy, and

the Strategic Logic of Anti-Foreign Protest" (Ph.D. dissertation, University of California–San Diego, 2008); Peter Hays Gries, "China's 'New Thinking' on Japan," *China Quarterly* 184 (2005).

12. Even under Mao Zedong when the Communist victory over the Japanese was emphasized, popular narratives through books and films continued to be about Japanese exploitation and China's suffering.

13. Finnemore and Sikkink, "International Norm Dynamics and Political Change."

14. Ayoob, "The Third World in the System of States."

15. Historians legitimately dispute the occurrence of some of these episodes.

16. Amartya Sen, "Starvation and Exchange Entitlements: General Approach and Its Application to the Great Bengal Famine," *Cambridge Journal of Economics* 1, no. 1 (1977): 33–59. As an example of how this history is passed on through stories and anecdotes told to children, I remember my Calcutta born-and-bred mother telling me a heart-wrenching story about the famine that my maternal grandmother had passed down to her. During the Bengal famine, rice was so scarce that people would beg at their door, not for a little rice but for a little "phan"—the foam that collects on top of the water when rice is boiled.

17. G. K. Ghosh and S. Ghosh, *Indian Textiles: Past and Present* (New Delhi: S. B. Nangia, 1995), 161.

18. These are disputed. But, nevertheless, children grow up hearing the stories.

Chapter 1

1. Apart from the broader application of the concept, the term "post-imperial" rather than "post-colonial" was chosen to distinguish my theory from the post-colonial literature.

2. As I will discuss in the chapter, my theory is concerned with extractive rather than settler colonialism.

3. While the words "colonialism" and "trauma" have been used in similar contexts, sometimes even in the same sentence, there is no treatment of it in its entirety as collective trauma, the way the Holocaust, for example, has been treated as trauma. Rather, specific events and instances of colonialism have been classified as traumatic, such as the trauma inflicted on Native Americans or aborigines by colonial settlers, or the Nanjing Massacre. The work that has approached closest to framing colonialism as trauma is Frantz Fanon's classic *The Wretched of the Earth*.

4. The word "event" is used as a way to best categorize the collective phenomenon of imperialism and colonialism. It is not a denial of the historical and temporal variations within colonial experiences. Indeed, this book uses the cases of India and China, which have vastly different colonial histories.

5. J. A. Hobson, *Imperialism: A Study* (London: Allen and Unwin, 1968); Vladimir Lenin, *Imperialism: The Highest Stage of Capitalism* (Moscow: Foreign Languages Publishing House, 1920); Michael Doyle, *Empires* (Ithaca, NY: Cornell University Press, 1986).

6. Doyle, *Empires*; Edward Said, *Culture and Imperialism* (New York: Knopf, Distributed by Random House, 1993).

7. Daron Acemoglu, Simon Johnson and James Robinson, *The Colonial Origins of*

Comparative Development (Cambridge, MA: National Bureau of Economic Research, 2000).

8. Robert Jackson, "The Weight of Ideas in Decolonization," in *Ideas and Foreign Policy: Beliefs, Institutions, and Political Change*, ed. J. Goldstein and R. Keohane (Ithaca, NY: Cornell University Press, 1993), 114.

9. Ibid.

10. Neta Crawford, *Argument and Change in World Politics* (New York: Cambridge University Press, 2002), 138.

11. Robert Jackson, *Quasi-States: Sovereignty, International Relations, and the Third World* (New York: Cambridge University Press, 1990), 85.

12. The English East India Company became the British East India Company when the Acts of Union joined the Kingdom of England and Kingdom of Scotland into Great Britain in 1707.

13. Sugata Bose and Ayesha Jalal, eds., *Modern South Asia: History, Culture, Political Economy* (New York: Oxford University Press, 2004), 18.

14. Ashin Dasgupta, quoted in ibid., 34.

15. S. C. M. Paine, *Imperial Rivals: China, Russia, and Their Disputed Frontier* (Armonk, NY: M. E. Sharpe, 1996), 9.

16. Ibid.

17. Mark Mancall, *China at the Center: 300 Years of Foreign Policy* (New York: Free Press, 1984), 71.

18. Ibid., 90.

19. John Fairbank and Merle Goldman, *China: A New History* (Cambridge, MA: Belknap Press of Harvard University Press, 1998), 198.

20. Ibid., 198–99.

21. Mancall, *China at the Center*, 117.

22. Fairbank and Goldman, *China*, 201.

23. Mancall, *China at the Center*, 285.

24. Ministry of Foreign Affairs, Republic of Indonesia, 1955, 36.

25. Laurence Kirmayer, Robert Lemelson and Mark Barad, eds., *Understanding Trauma: Integrating Biological, Clinical, and Cultural Perspectives* (New York: Cambridge University Press, 2007), 1.

26. Judith Herman, *Trauma and Recovery* (New York: Basic Books, 1992), 33.

27. M. A. Gagné, "The Role of Dependency and Colonialism in Generating Trauma in First Nations Citizens," in *International Handbook of Multigenerational Legacies of Trauma*, ed. Y. Danieli (New York: Plenum Press, 1998), 356.

28. American Psychiatric Association, *Diagnostic and Statistical Manual of Mental Disorders (DSM-III-R)*, 3rd ed. (Washington, DC: American Psychiatric Association, 1987).

29. Kirmayer, Lemelson and Barad, *Understanding Trauma*, 2.

30. Leslie Dwyer and Degung Santikarma, "Post-traumatic Politics: Violence, Memory and Biomedical Discourse in Bali," in *Understanding Trauma*, ed. L. Kirmayer, R. Lemelson and M. Barad (New York: Cambridge University Press, 2007), 405.

31. Jeffrey Alexander et al., *Toward a Theory of Cultural Trauma* (Berkeley: University of California Press, 2004), 4; Kirmayer, Lemelson and Barad, *Understanding Trauma*, 5.

32. Kirmayer, Lemelson and Barad, *Understanding Trauma*, 10; Judy Atkinson, *Trauma Trails: Recreating Song Lines* (North Melbourne, Vic.: Spinifex Press, 2002).

33. Alexander, *Toward a Theory of Cultural Trauma*, 1.

34. Neil Smelser, "Psychological Trauma and Cultural Trauma," in ibid., 36.

35. Ibid., 36–38.

36. Neil Smelser, "Epilogue: September 11, 2001, as Cultural Trauma," in *Toward a Theory of Cultural Trauma*.

37. Dwyer and Santikarma, "Post-traumatic Politics."

38. Ibid., 37.

39. Ibid., 37–38.

40. Richard McNally, *Remembering Trauma* (Cambridge: Belknap Press of Harvard University Press, 2003), 28.

41. Daniel Schacter, *Searching for Memory: The Brain, the Mind, and the Past* (New York: Basic Books, 1996), 7.

42. Daniel Schacter, "Implicit Memory: History and Current Status," *Journal of Experimental Psychology* 13 (1987): 501.

43. James Wertsch, *Voices of Collective Remembering* (New York: Cambridge University Press, 2002), 152.

44. J. M. Winter and Emmanuel Sivan, *War and Remembrance in the Twentieth Century* (New York: Cambridge University Press, 1999), 7.

45. McNally, *Remembering Trauma*, 77, 84.

46. Green (1990), quoted in ibid., 78.

47. Wertsch, *Voices of Collective Remembering*, 152.

48. Ibid., 7, 33–35.

49. Allan Young, "Bruno and the Holy Fool: Myth, Mimesis and the Transmission of Traumatic Memories," in *Understanding Trauma*, 339.

50. Ibid., 342.

51. Alexander, *Toward a Theory of Cultural Trauma*, 8.

52. Winter and Sivan, *War and Remembrance in the Twentieth Century*, 16.

53. Max Weber, *Economy and Society*, ed. Guenther Roth and Claus Wittich (New York: Bedminster Press, 1968), 468–517, quoted in Alexander, *Toward a Theory of Cultural Trauma*, 11.

54. Ibid.

55. Winter and Sivan, *War and Remembrance in the Twentieth Century*, 17; Alexander, *Toward a Theory of Cultural Trauma*, 11.

56. John Sigal and M. Weinfeld, *Trauma and Rebirth: Intergenerational Effects of the Holocaust* (New York: Praeger, 1989); Nanette Auerhahn and Dori Laub, "Intergenerational Memory of the Holocaust," in *International Handbook of Multigenerational Legacies of Trauma*, 21–42; Zahava Solomon, "Transgenerational Effects of the Holocaust," in *International Handbook of Multigenerational Legacies of Trauma*, 69–84; Gagné, "The Role of Dependency."

57. Sigal and Weinfeld, *Trauma and Rebirth*, 1.

58. Auerhahn and Laub, "Intergenerational Memory of the Holocaust," 39; Solomon, "Transgenerational Effects of the Holocaust," 69.

59. Atkinson, *Trauma Trails*; Gagné, "The Role of Dependency."

60. Alexander, *Toward a Theory of Cultural Trauma*, 1, 3.

61. Arthur Neal, *National Trauma and Collective Memory: Major Events in the American Century* (Armonk, NY: M. E. Sharpe, 1998), 4.

62. Ibid., 7.

63. William Dalrymple, *The Last Mughal: The Fall of a Dynasty* (New York: Alfred A. Knopf, 2007).

64. Sumit Sarkar, *A Critique of Colonial India* (Calcutta, India: Papyrus, 1985), 43.

65. "The Condition of India," speech given by Dadabhai Naoroji, Toynbee Hall, Commercial Street, Whitechapel E., Thursday night, 31 January 1901. In *Speeches and Writings of Dadabhai Naoroji 1825–1917* (Madras, India: Natesan and Co., 1909), 226–28.

66. "The Causes of Discontent," submitted by Dadabhai Naoroji to the Welby Commission, 31 January 1897. In ibid., 375, 380–81.

67. Michael Mann, "Dealing with Oriental Despotism: British Jurisdiction in Bengal, 1772–93," in *Colonialism as Civilizing Mission: Cultural Ideology in British India*, ed. Harald Fischer-Tiné and Michael Mann (London: Anthem Press, 2004), 18; Ranajit Guha, *Dominance without Hegemony: History and Power in Colonial India* (Cambridge: Harvard University Press, 1997).

68. "The Causes of Discontent": submitted by Dadabhai Naoroji to the Welby Commission, 31 January 1897. In *Speeches and Writings of Dadabhai Naoroji*, 382.

69. Robert Bickers, *Britain in China: Community, Culture, and Colonialism, 1900–1949* (New York: Manchester University Press, 1999), 9.

70. Hu Sheng, *Diguo Zhuyi Yu Zhongguo Zhengzhi* (Beijing: Ren Min Chubanshe, 1955); Ding Mingnan et al., *Diguo Zhuyi Qinhua Shi* (Beijing: Kexue Chubanshe, 1958); San Benren and Pan Xingming, *Ershi Shiji De Zhong Ying Guanxi* (Shanghai: Shanghai People's Publishing, 1996).

71. Robert Lee, *France and the Exploitation of China, 1885–1901: A Study in Economic Imperialism* (New York: Oxford University Press, 1989); Guangsheng Liao, *Antiforeignism and Modernization in China, 1860–1980: Linkage between Domestic Politics and Foreign Policy* (New York: St. Martin's Press, 1984); Bickers, *Britain in China*.

72. Hu Sheng, *Diguo Zhuyi Yu Zhongguo Zhengzhi*, 7.

73. Bickers, *Britain in China*, 68, 72, 76, 83.

74. Ibid., 73, 81.

75. Robert Bickers and R. G. Tiedman, *The Boxers, China, and the World* (Lanham: Rowman and Littlefield, 2007), xvii.

76. Contrary to expectations, until the early 1990s, television in India was entirely controlled by the state. The press, however, was free.

77. Jackson, *Quasi-States*, 85.

78. Mark Ashley, "Nations as Victims: Nationalist Politics and the Framing of Identity," paper prepared for delivery at the 2001 Annual Meeting of the American Political Science Association, San Francisco, 30 August–2 September 2001.

79. Quoted in Suhasini Haidar, "Apology over 'Strip-Search' Saga," *CNN.com*, 14 July 2004.

80. Robert Scalapino, "China's Multiple Identities in East Asia: China as a Regional

Force," in *China's Quest for National Identity*, ed. L. Dittmer and S. Kim (Ithaca, NY: Cornell University Press, 1993), 217.

81. Andrew Nathan and Robert Ross, *The Great Wall and Empty Fortress: China's Search for Security* (New York: W. W. Norton, 1997), 26, 29–33.

82. Ibid., 34.

83. Peter Gries, "Tears of Rage: Chinese Nationalist Reactions to the Belgrade Embassy Bombing," *China Journal* 46 (July 2001): 26.

84. A. Katyal, "Cong Defends Manmohan's Oxford Speech," *The Tribune*, 9 July 2005.

85. Sugata Bose, *A Hundred Horizons: The Indian Ocean in the Age of Global Empire* (Cambridge: Harvard University Press, 2006), 63.

86. Ibid., 55–56.

87. Ibid.

88. Paine, *Imperial Rivals*, 50.

89. Allen Carlson, "Constructing a New Great Wall: Chinese Foreign Policy and the Norm of State Sovereignty" (Ph.D. dissertation, Yale University, 2000), 41.

90. Bose and Jalal, *Modern South Asia*, 30.

91. C. A. Bayly, *Indian Society and the Making of the British Empire* (New York: Cambridge University Press, 2002), 13.

92. Amitav Acharya, conversation with author, Cambridge, MA, November 2004.

93. Alastair Iain Johnston, "International Structures and Chinese Foreign Policy," in *China and the World: Chinese Foreign Policy Faces the New Millennium*, ed. S. Kim (Boulder, CO: Westview Press, 1998), 73.

94. Carlson, "Constructing a New Great Wall," 5.

95. J. N. Dixit (former foreign secretary, former national security adviser to the government of India), interview with author, New Delhi, India, March 2004.

96. Daniel Markey, "The Prestige Motive in International Relations" (Ph.D. dissertation, Princeton University, 2000).

97. Quoted in Amitav Acharya, "Why Is There No NATO in Asia? Norms, Institution-Building, and Security Cooperation in Asian Regionalism," 8. Paper presented at the Weatherhead Center for International Affairs seminar, November 2004, Harvard University, Cambridge, MA.

98. Bose and Jalal, *Modern South Asia*, 90.

99. Partha Chatterjee, *The Nation and Its Fragments: Colonial and Postcolonial Histories* (Princeton: Princeton University Press, 1993), 6.

100. Nathan and Ross, *The Great Wall and Empty Fortress*, 26, 29–33.

101. Paine, *Imperial Rivals*, 9.

102. William Callahan, "National Insecurities: Humiliation, Salvation, and Chinese Nationalism," *Alternatives* 29, no. 2 (2004): 205.

103. Johnston, "International Structures and Chinese Foreign Policy," 75.

104. J. N. Dixit and S. K. Singh (former foreign secretary), interviews with author, New Delhi, India, March 2004. Confirmed independently by both.

105. William Callahan, "History, Identity and Security: Producing and Consuming Nationalism in China," *Critical Asian Studies* 38, no. 2 (2006).

106. Ibid., 180.

107. See, for example, "India Pokhran Tests Meant to End Nuclear Apartheid," *The Hindu*, 6 September 1998; "A Repudiation of Nuclear Apartheid Policy," *The Hindu*, 12 May 1998; "Struggling to Get a Grip," *Indian Express*, 9 July 1998; "Time to Stand Firm," *Financial Express*, 28 May 1998.

108. Martha Finnemore and Kathryn Sikkink, "International Norm Dynamics and Political Change," *International Organization* 52, no. 4 (1998): 887–917.

109 Mohammed Ayoob, "The Third World in the System of States: Acute Schizophrenia or Growing Pains?" *International Studies Quarterly* 33, no. 1 (March 1989): 68.

Chapter 2

1. This is the standard method of content analysis.

2. Sydney Bailey, *The General Assembly of the United Nations: A Study of Procedure and Practice* (Westport, CT: Greenwood Press, 1978), 70.

3. Ibid.

4. I would like to acknowledge and thank Dr. Jeffrey Burnham Miller. Without his use of Igor software and help on the statistical analysis this research would not have been possible.

5. In addition to these members, Palestine has been participating in the General Debate since 1998. In addition to Palestine, the Holy See has also occasionally made speeches during the Debate.

6. Thanks to Paul Hensel. The dataset was downloaded from his webpage at http://garnet.acns.fsu.edu/~phensel/icowdata.html#colonies.

7. Hensel's dataset has four types of colonialism. Type 1 is a colony/dependency where the possessor controlled most/all of the entity; Type 2 is a colony/dependency where the possessor controlled part of the entity; Type 3 is occupation where the possessor occupies the entity militarily but does not rule it as a colony; Type 4 is a League of Nations mandate or a UN trusteeship. The types were merged into two categories depending primarily on whether the state had been an extractive colony.

8. There are 1,655 speeches made by C_1 states and 511 speeches made by C_2 states.

9. There were 35,715 different words used in the speeches. Some 16,323 words were thrown out, which is about 46 percent of the total dictionary. The remaining 19,392 words were used in at least three different speeches.

10. For example, suppose C_1 states use a particular word three times more than C_2 states, thus $f_i^{C_1} = 3 f_i^{C_2}$. Then $D_i = \log f_i^{C_1} - \log f_i^{C_2} = \log 3 f_i^{C_2} - \log f_i^{C_2} = \log 3 + \log f_i^{C_2} - \log f_i^{C_2} = \log 3 = 0.48$.

11. In fact, I have done extensive studies of histograms of D_i, and have confirmed that a histogram methodology does give identical results to the preferred method of probability density functions (PDF). The difficulty of selecting bins and the inherent discretization noise of histograms makes the PDF method preferable.

12. The fact that there are always the same number of states in each C_1^* (as in C_1) and the same number of states in each C_2^* (as in C_2) automatically accounts for any biases that could be caused by the fact that C_1 contains more states than C_2.

13. I am not claiming that PII is the only contributor to these differences in word usage but that the categorization of states by colonial status does lead to enhanced differences in word usage.

Chapter 3

Portions of this chapter previously appeared as "Re-collecting Empire: 'Victimhood' and the 1962 Sino-Indian War," *Asian Security* 5, issue 3 (2009): 216–41, and have been reprinted by permission of Taylor & Francis.

1.   Ministry of External Affairs, Government of India, 1961, 233, CR-186.

2.   Mao Tse-Tung to Jawaharlal Nehru, 24 May 1939, J. N. Papers, Vol. 45, Nehru Memorial Library, New Delhi, India.

3.   Herbert Passin, "Sino-Indian Cultural Relations," *China Quarterly* 7 (July–September 1961): 85.

4.   Ibid., 96.

5.   The Indian and Chinese governments have declassified very few documents (and none of much significance) pertaining to the border dispute. This private collection, however, includes detailed verbatim transcripts of the 1960 border negotiations between Zhou Enlai and Jawaharlal Nehru, as well as dispatches between top Indian government officials and the Indian embassy in Beijing analyzing the situation. The only other published (and cursory) reference to these documents is in Ramachandra Guha's *India after Gandhi: The History of the World's Largest Democracy* (New York: HarperCollins, 2007), where he notes that the transcripts of the talks between Zhou and Nehru are still officially secret.

6.   There were also problems in the middle sector of the frontier, which ran from the Indian state of Uttar Pradesh to Punjab, but this squabble was peripheral to the main conflict.

7.   Steven Hoffmann, *India and the China Crisis* (Berkeley: University of California Press, 1990), 12.

8.   Ibid., 15.

9.   Ibid., 16.

10.   Neville Maxwell, *India's China War* (London: Cape, 1970), 48.

11.   Ibid., 174–75.

12.   John K. Fairbank, *China Watch* (Cambridge: Harvard University Press, 1987).

13.   Allen S. Whiting, *Chinese Calculus of Deterrence: India and Indochina* (Ann Arbor: University of Michigan Press, 1975), 12.

14.   Ibid., 14.

15.   Yaacov Vertzberger, "India's Border Conflict with China: A Perceptual Analysis," *Journal of Contemporary History* 17, no. 4 (October 1982): 607.

16.   Hoffmann, *India and the China Crisis*, 48.

17.   John W. Garver, "China's Decision for War with India in 1962," in *New Directions in the Study of China's Foreign Policy*, ed. A. I. Johnston and R. Ross (Palo Alto, CA: Stanford University Press, 2006), 86–130.

18.   Judith Brown, *Nehru: A Political Life* (New Haven: Yale University Press, 2003), 322.

19.   M. Taylor Fravel, "Regime Insecurity and International Cooperation: Explaining China's Compromises in Territorial Disputes," *International Security* 30, no. 2 (2005): 68.

20.   Whiting, *Chinese Calculus of Deterrence*, 11.

21.   Papers that are supposedly declassified are notoriously hard to obtain in hard copy.

22. Kuan-Hsing Chen and Hee-Yeon Cho, *Bandung/Third Worldism* (Abingdon: Routledge, 2005), 473.

23. Partha Chatterjee, "Empire and Nation Revisited: 50 Years after Bandung," *Inter-Asia Cultural Studies* 6, no. 4 (2005): 488.

24. Brown, *Nehru*, 246.

25. Jawaharlal Nehru, *Selected Works of Jawaharlal Nehru,* Vol. 28 (1 February–31 May 1955) (New Delhi: Jawaharlal Nehru Memorial Fund, 2001), 99.

26. Ibid. (22 April 1955), 109.

27. Five Principles of Peaceful Co-Existence.

28. Paul F. Power, "Indian Foreign Policy: The Age of Nehru," *Review of Politics* 26, no. 2 (1964): 258.

29. Brown, *Nehru*, 256.

30. J. N. Dixit (former foreign secretary and national security advisor) and S. K. Singh (former foreign secretary and governor of Arunachal Pradesh and Rajasthan), interviews with author, New Delhi, India, March 2004. Confirmed independently by both.

31. See Nehru, *Selected Works,* Vol. 28.

32. Ibid. (8 February 1955), 166.

33. Ibid. (27 March 1955), 177.

34. Ibid., 181–82.

35. Ibid. (24 April 1955), 127.

36. Ibid. (28 April 1955), 136.

37. Ibid. (3 May 1955), 154.

38. Harold Vinacke, "Communist China and the Uncommitted Zone," *Annals of the American Academy of Political and Social Science* 362 (1965): 114.

39. Ibid., 115.

40. *Asia-Africa Speaks from Bandung* (Jakarta: Ministry of Foreign Affairs, Republic of Indonesia, 1955), 57, 59.

41. William Holland, *Selected Documents of the Bandung Conference: Texts of Selected Speeches and Final Communique of the Asian-African Conference, Bandung Indonesia, April 18–24, 1955* (New York: Institute of Pacific Relations, 1955), 21–22.

42. Vinacke, "Communist China and the Uncommitted Zone"; Kuo-kang Shao, "Chou En Lai's Diplomatic Approach to Non-Aligned States in Asia: 1953–1960," *China Quarterly* 78 (June 1979): 324–28.

43. Peter Poole, "Communist China's Aid Diplomacy," *Asian Survey* 6, no. 11 (November 1966): 622.

44. Cambodia was the first state to benefit, followed by Indonesia in 1956, when the Chinese agreed to fund Indonesia's $16 million trade deficit, Sri Lanka and Nepal. After Egypt recognized the PRC in 1956, it received a grant of $4.7 million in hard currency during the Suez crisis. In 1959, aid agreements led to close ties with sub-Saharan Africa when a shipment of rice was donated to the Republic of Guinea (ibid., 624–25).

45. The transcripts were the Indian government's version of the discussions. It is not entirely clear whether they are based on recordings or from Indian note takers.

46. Meeting between PM Nehru and Premier Chou, 5:00 p.m., 20 April 1960, 5, Subject File 26, Installment I/II, P. N. Haksar private papers, Nehru Memorial Library Archives, New Delhi, India.

47. Ibid., 8.

48. Ibid. (10:00 a.m., 22 April 1960), 4.

49. Ibid., 7.

50. Whiting, *Chinese Calculus of Deterrence*, referred to the strategic importance of Aksai China to Xinjiang, and I agree with his analysis. However, I disagree that the emphasis on Xinjiang was only because the Chinese felt it was vital to state security.

51. P. N. Haksar private papers (4:00 p.m., 21 April 1960), 4.

52. Ibid. (5:00 p.m., 20 April 1960), 7.

53. Peter Perdue, *China Marches West: The Qing Conquest of Central Eurasia* (Cambridge: Belknap Press of Harvard University, 2005), 333.

54. Ibid., 334–35.

55. Melvyn Goldstein, *The Snow Lion and the Dragon: China, Tibet, and the Dalai Lama* (Berkeley: University of California Press, 1997), 24–25.

56. P. N. Haksar private papers (5:00 p.m., 20 April 1960), 1–2.

57. Ministry of External Affairs, Government of India, 1961, CR-187.

58. Conversation between home minister and Premier Chou, 11:25 a.m., 21 April 1960, 10, SF 26.

59. P. B. Sinha, A. A. Athale and S. N. Prasad, eds., *History of the Conflict with China, 1962* (New Delhi: Ministry of Defence, Government of India, 1992) (published online in 2002 by the *Times of India*), 2.

60. Ibid.

61. Alastair Lamb, *The China-India Border* (London: Oxford University Press, 1964), 11.

62. Ibid.

63. Meeting between PM Nehru and Premier Chou (4:30 p.m., 23 April 1960), 7.

64. Ibid., 1–2, 4.

65. Ibid. (4:00 p.m., 21 April 1960), 2.

66. Ibid., 8.

67. Ibid. (10:00 a.m., 22 April 1960), 2–3.

68. Ibid., 5–7.

69. Ibid. (10:00 a.m., 20 April 1960), 4.

70. Prime Minister's Reply to Lok Sabha Discussions, Subject File 25. P. N. Haksar private papers (Nehru Memorial Library Archives, New Delhi, India), 22 February 1960.

71. Prem Nath Dogra (Jammu and Kashmir Praja Parishad) to Jawaharlal Nehru, 17 April 1960, Subject File 25, Installment I/II, P. N. Haksar private papers, Nehru Memorial Library Archives, New Delhi, India.

72. Meeting between Finance Minister and Premier Chou (22 April 1960), 1, SF 26.

73. Ibid., 6.

74. Telegram from Foreign Secretary Dutt to Indian ambassador Parthasarathy, 20 March 1960, SF 25.

75. Telegram from Indian ambassador Parthasarathy to Foreign Secretary Dutt (exact date is unclear but is in response to Dutt's telegram of 20 March), March 1960, SF 25.

76. Meeting between PM Nehru and Premier Chou (10:00 a.m., 22 April 1960), 2.

77. Ibid. (5:00 p.m., 20 April 1960), 3.

78. Ibid., 1.

79. Ibid., 3, 6–7, 9.

80. Ibid. (10:00 a.m., 22 April 1960), 4.

81. Ibid. (10:30 a.m., 24 April 1960), 6.

82. Telegram from Foreign Secretary to Heads of Mission, 27 April 1960, 2, SF 25.

83. Meeting between PM Nehru and Premier Chou (5:00 p.m., 20 April 1960), 8.

84. Ibid. (4:00 p.m., 21 April 1960), 6.

85. Ibid. (10:00 a.m., 22 April 1960), 10.

86. Telegram from Indian Embassy in Beijing to Foreign Secretary, 27 April 1960, 1, SF 25.

87. Nehru, *Selected Works,* Vol. 28 (22 April 1955), 107.

Chapter 4

1. Raj Chengappa, *Weapons of Peace: The Secret Story of India's Quest to Be a Nuclear Power* (New Delhi: Harper Collins India, 2000), 58.

2. For detailed histories of India's nuclear program, see Ashok Kapur, *India's Nuclear Option: Atomic Diplomacy and Decision Making* (New York: Praeger, 1976); Shyam Bhatia, *India's Nuclear Bomb* (Sahibabad, Distt. Ghaziabad: Vikas, 1979); and George Perkovich, *India's Nuclear Bomb: The Impact on Nuclear Proliferation* (Berkeley: University of California Press, 1999).

3. Sumit Ganguly, "India's Pathway to Pokhran II: The Prospects and Sources of New Delhi's Nuclear Weapons Program," *International Security* 23, no. 4 (1999): 150.

4. A resolution of the party's General Working Committee on 4 December 1964 stated, "The Working Committee, therefore, considers it imperative that an all out effort be made to build up an independent nuclear deterrent . . . and urges the government of India to revise its stand accordingly." Quoted in Bhatia, *India's Nuclear Bomb*, 112.

5. Bhumitra Chakma, "Toward Pokhran II: Explaining India's Nuclearisation Process," *Modern Asian Studies* 39, no. 1 (February 2005): 210.

6. D. R. SarDesai and Raju Thomas, *Nuclear India in the Twenty-First Century* (New York: Palgrave, 2002), 6.

7. Perkovich, *India's Nuclear Bomb*, 33.

8. Ibid., 34.

9. "The House of the People," or the lower house of the Indian Parliament.

10. The core of this ideology is right-wing Hindu nationalism positing the greatness of the Hindu nation. Interestingly and not coincidentally, the ancient Hindu texts, idolized by the BJP, talk of the *Brahmastra,* the ultimate weapon of mass destruction—"It was a single projectile/Charged with all the power of the Universe/An incandescent column of smoke and flame/As bright as ten thousand suns/Rose in all its splendor/It was an unknown weapon/An iron thunderbolt/A gigantic messenger of death/Endowed with the force/Of thousand-eyed Indra's thunder/It was destructive of all living creatures (*Mahabharata*, circa 900–1500 B.C.).

11. The text of Prime Minister Vajpayee's announcement of nuclear tests, 11 May 1998. Available online at http://www.indianembassy.org/pic/vajpayee1198.htm.

12. Chengappa, *Weapons of Peace*, xv.

13. "Most Indians Hail N-Tests," *The Hindu*, 12 May 1998.

14. "Nuclear Anxiety: The Blunders: US Blundered on Intelligence, Officials Admit," *New York Times*, 13 May 1998.

15. "Stoicism It'll Have to Be," *Indian Express*, 23 July 1998.

16. Scott Sagan, "Why Do States Build Nuclear Weapons?: Three Models in Search of a Bomb," *International Security* 21, no. 3 (1996–97): 54–86.

17. Ibid., 55.

18. Ashley Tellis, *India's Emerging Nuclear Posture: Between Recessed Deterrent and Ready Arsenal* (Santa Monica, CA: RAND, 2001); K. Subrahmanyam, "India and the International Nuclear Order," in *Nuclear India in the Twenty-First Century*, ed. SarDesai and Thomas, 63–84; Chakma, "Toward Pokhran II"; Jasjit Singh, *Nuclear India* (New Delhi: Knowledge World in association with the Institute for Defence Studies and Analyses, 1998); and Amitabh Mattoo, *India's Nuclear Deterrent: Pokhran II and Beyond* (New Delhi: Har-Anand, 1999).

19. "George in the China Shop," *India Today*, 18 May 1998.

20. Quoted in Perkovich, *India's Nuclear Bomb*, 417.

21. T. V. Paul, "India, the International System and Nuclear Weapons," in *Nuclear India in the Twenty-First Century*, ed. SarDesai and Thomas, 88.

22. Ibid., 90.

23. Achin Vanaik, "The Indian Nuclear Tests: Causes, Consequences and Portents," *Comparative Studies of South Asia, Africa and the Middle East* 18, no. 1 (1998). The concept of the scientific-bureaucratic community pushing for tests has been emphasized by Perkovich, *India's Nuclear Bomb*; and by Itty Abraham, *The Making of the Indian Atomic Bomb: Science, Secrecy, and the Postcolonial State* (London: Zed Books, 1998).

24. "National Parties: Jai Shri Bomb!," *India Today*, 1 June 1998.

25. Perkovich, *India's Nuclear Bomb*, 34.

26. Siddharth Srivastava, "Onion Prices Bring Tears to India's Eyes," *Asia Times*, 14 February 2007.

27. Jacques Hymans, "Why Do States Acquire Nuclear Weapons? Comparing the Cases of India and France," in *Nuclear India in the Twenty-First Century*, ed. SarDesai and Thomas, 143.

28. Quoted in SarDesai and Thomas, *Nuclear India in the Twenty-First Century*, 19.

29. Alastair Iain Johnston, "Is China a Status Quo Power?," *International Security* 27, no. 4 (Spring 2003): 5–56.

30. Hymans, "Why Do States Acquire Nuclear Weapons?," 144–45.

31. Ibid.

32. Jacques Hymans, *The Psychology of Nuclear Proliferation: Identity, Emotions and Foreign Policy* (New York: Cambridge University Press, 2006), 198.

33. Ibid.

34. J. N. Dixit, "Jawaharlal Nehru: Architect of India's Foreign Policy," in *Nehru Revisited*, ed. V. Kamath (Mumbai: Nehru Centre, 2003), 65.

35. Ibid., 66–67.

36. India's refusal of a permanent seat on the UN Security Council as part of its principled opposition to the PRC's UN seat being given to the ROC is an example of that. See Chapter 1.

37. Stephen Cohen, *India: Emerging Power* (Washington, DC: Brookings Institution Press, 2001), 161.

38. Bharat Karnad, *Nuclear Weapons and Indian Security: The Realist Foundations of Strategy* (New Delhi: Macmillan, 2002), 182, 199.

39. Bhatia, *India's Nuclear Bomb*, 42.

40. In 1954, a Japanese fishing boat was affected by radioactive fallout and Nehru sent a statement to the UN Secretary General (Ibid., 56).

41. Ibid., 69.

42. Ibid., 115–18.

43. A. G. Noorani, "India's Quest for a Nuclear Guarantee," *Asian Survey* 7, no. 7 (1967): 492.

44. Ibid., 495.

45. Perkovich, *India's Nuclear Bomb*, 29.

46. U.S. analysts put it at less—somewhere between four and six kilotons. Ibid., 182.

47. Ibid., 170.

48. K. Subrahmanyam, "Indian Nuclear Policy 1964–98," in *Nuclear India*, ed. Jasjit Singh (New Delhi: Knowledge World in association with Institute for Defence Studies and Analyses, 1998), 30.

49. The government declared that Operation Smiling Buddha was a "peaceful nuclear explosion experiment" permitted under Article 5 of the 1970 NPT (SarDesai and Thomas, *Nuclear India in the Twenty-First Century*, 6; Perkovich, *India's Nuclear Bomb*, 178).

50. Cohen, *India*, 42.

51. Nandan Nilekani, *Imagining India: The Idea of a Renewed Nation* (New York: Penguin, 2009), 67–68.

52. Ibid., 31.

53. Although these comparisons did not become ubiquitous until after 9/11.

54. See Johnston's definitions 2 and 3 of a non–status quo power in "Is China a Status Quo Power?," 11.

55. Term used by Bharat Karnad.

56. Perkovich, *India's Nuclear Bomb*, 127.

57. Ibid., 134.

58. Ibid., 138.

59. Ibid., 134.

60. See, for example, Singh, *Nuclear India*; Subrahmanyam, "India and the International Nuclear Order," 67; SarDesai and Thomas, *Nuclear India in the Twenty-First Century*, 8; "India Pokhran Tests Meant to End Nuclear Apartheid," *The Hindu*, 6 September 1998; "A Repudiation of Nuclear Apartheid Policy," *The Hindu*, 12 May 1998; "Struggling to Get a Grip," *Indian Express*, 9 July 1998; "Time to Stand Firm," *Financial Express*, 28 May 1998.

61. Subrahmanyam, "India and the International Nuclear Order," 66.

62. Ibid., 66–67.

63. Quoted in Perkovich, *India's Nuclear Bomb*, 379.

64. Ibid., 383.

65. The UK and France ratified it on 6 April 1998, Russia on 30 June 2000.

66. Geeta Puri, "Between Identity and Power," *Indian Express*, 3 June 1999.

67. Chengappa, *Weapons of Peace*, 35–36.

68. Complete BJP 1998 Election Manifesto available at http://www.bjp.org/content/view/2626/428.

69. Ibid.

70. Ibid.

71. Quoted in Chengappa, *Weapons of Peace*, 36.

72. "No Soviet N-Test in Indian Ocean," *Indian Express*, 18 January 1974.

73. "Delhi Calls for Talks on Indian Ocean Moves," *Indian Express*, 13 March 1974; "Foreign Naval Base in Indian Ocean Will Cause Tension," *Indian Express*, 1 April 1974; "US to Send Ships to Match Soviet Fleet in Ocean," *Indian Express*, 1 April 1974.

74. "Nuclear Arms," Letter to the editor, *Indian Express*, 18 January 1974.

75. "Thrilled Nation Hails Atomic Scientists," *Indian Express*, 19 May 1974.

76. "Grudging Respect for India in USA," *Indian Express*, 20 May 1974.

77. "N-Explosion Has Upset US Military Applecart," *Indian Express*, 21 May 1974; "The Political Fallout," *Indian Express*, 22 May 1974.

78. "India: No Pawn of Any Nation: Samar Sen," *Indian Express*, 22 May 1974.

79. "Inches Taller," *Indian Express*, 20 May 1974; "India Not Agreeable to Discriminatory Nuclear Treaty," *Indian Express*, 11 July 1974.

80. "India's Awesome Responsibility," *Indian Express*, 20 May 1974.

81. "US Efforts at NPT Run into Rough Weather," *Indian Express*, 17 January 1995; "N-options: Make the Stand Clear," *Indian Express*, 16 February 1995; "All Nuclear Weapons Must Be Abolished, Says Study," *Indian Express*, 2 March 1995; "US Initiative May Get No Takers at NPT Meet," *Indian Express*, 3 March 1995.

82. "Non-proliferation Treaty: Bad Past, No Future," *Indian Express*, 12 February 1995; "What Is at Stake?," *Indian Express*, 16 March 1995; "US Double Standards Threaten NPT Future," *Indian Express*, 2 March 1995.

83. "Asian Security Demands a Pro-active Approach," *Indian Express*, 10 January 1995; "US Braces Up for Arm Twisting as NPT Meet Begins," *Indian Express*, 18 April 1995; "NPT Passage to Increase Pressure on India," *Indian Express*, 13 May 1995.

84. "US Charges India with 'Greed' on Test Ban Treaty," *Indian Express*, 10 March 1996; "India Painted a Spoiler in a 'Perfect' World," *Indian Express*, 23 May 1996.

85. "Pugwash Joins the Gang to Pressurize India on CTBT," *Indian Express*, 24 February 1996; "Nuclear Blackmail Spearheads Assault on Indian Policy," *Indian Express*, 27 May 1996; "West's Bid to Make India Buckle on CTBT Issue," *Indian Express*, 18 June 1996; "US to Insist on India Joining Ban," *Indian Express*, 19 June 1996; "Russia Too Turns the Heat on India," *Indian Express*, 26 June 1996; "CTBT: Search for a Scapegoat Goes into Fast Lane," *Indian Express*, 27 June 1996; "UK Broadside on India Stuns Delegates," *Indian Express*, 28 June 1996; "The Dark Hands behind CTBT Closing In on India," *Indian Express*, 14 July 1996; "India Not to Succumb to US Pressure on CTBT: Gujral," *Indian Express*, 13 August 1996; "Nation Must Resist Pressures from Abroad, Says President," *Indian Express*, 15 August 1996; "Americans Must Learn to Take No for an Answer," *Indian Express*, 1 September 1996.

86. "Russia Too Turns the Heat on India," *Indian Express*, 26 June 1996.

87. "Pokharan '98: India Flexes Nuclear Muscle," *Indian Express*, 12 May 1998.

88. "Yes, Buddha's Smile Is Infectious for Us All," *Indian Express*, 12 May 1998.

89. "The Great Indian Blasts: Looking for Motives," *Indian Express*, 14 May 1998.

90. "Gujral for Signing CTBT, Says West Is Hypocritical," *Indian Express*, 14 May 1998; "Bill, the Selective Bully," *Indian Express*, 15 May 1998.

91. "Bill, the Selective Bully," *Indian Express*, 15 May 1998.

Chapter 5

1. Ministry of Commerce, People's Republic of China, "Japan Trade Statistics in September of 2010," 12 November 2010, http://english.mofcom.gov.cn/aarticle/statistic/lanmubb/ASEAN/201102/20110207394418.html.

2. Yinan He, "History, Chinese Nationalism and the Emerging Sino-Japanese Conflict," *Journal of Contemporary China* 16, no. 50 (2007).

3. Jian Zhang, "The Influence of Chinese Nationalism on Sino-Japanese Relations," in *China-Japan Relations in the Twenty-First Century: Creating a Future Past?*, ed. Michael Heazle and Nick Knight (Northampton, MA: Edward Elgar, 2007), 17–19.

4. Yinan He, "Remembering and Forgetting the War: Elite Mythmaking, Mass Reaction, and Sino-Japanese Relations, 1950–2006," *History and Memory* 19, no. 2 (2007): 43–74.

5. India, Germany and Brazil were considered the other most likely candidates.

6. Parag Khanna, "One More Seat at the Table," *New York Times*, 6 December 2003.

7. James Traub, "The World According to China," *New York Times*, 3 September 2006.

8. Warren Hoge, "UN Report Urges Big Changes; Security Council Would Expand," *New York Times*, 1 December 2004.

9. J. Mohan Malik, "Security Council Reform: China Signals Its Veto," *World Policy Journal* 22, no. 1 (2005): 20.

10. Ibid.

11. Ibid.

12. Jin Xide, "Riben Lianheguo Waijiao de Dingwei yu Yanbian," *Shijie Jingji Yu Zhengzhi*, no. 5 (2005): 24.

13. Colum Lynch, "China Fights Enlarging UN Security Council," *Washington Post*, 5 April 2005.

14. Available online at http://www.chinadaily.com.cn/english/doc/2005-03/30/content_429243.htm.

15. Philip P. Pan, "Youth Attack Japan's Embassy in China; Historic, Territorial Disputes Fuel Protest; Witnesses Allege Official Support," *Washington Post*, 10 April 2005.

16. Jonathan Watts, "Violence Flares as the Chinese Rage at Japan," *The Guardian*, 17 April 2005.

17. Ibid.

18. Philip P. Pan, "Chinese Step Up Criticism of Japan; Premier Calls Tokyo Unfit for New Role on Security Council," *Washington Post*, 13 April 2005.

19. Ibid.

20. Ibid.

21. Geoffrey York, "Japan Tries to Mend Quarrel with China," *Friday's Globe and Mail*, 23 April 2005.

22. "China Says Japan Ties Worst in 30 Years, Affect Region," *Deutsche Presse-Agentur*, 18 April 2005.

23. June Teufel Dreyer, "Sino-Japanese Relations," *Journal of Contemporary China* 10, no. 28 (2001).

24. Xinbo Wu, "The Security Dimension of Sino-Japanese Relations: Warily Watching One Another," *Asian Survey* 40, no. 2 (2000).

25. Reinhard Drifte, *Japan's Security Relations with China since 1989: From Balancing to Bandwagoning?*, Nissan Institute/RoutledgeCurzon Japanese Studies Series (London, New York: RoutledgeCurzon, 2003).

26. Alastair Iain Johnston, "Is China a Status Quo Power?," *International Security* 27, no. 4 (Spring 2003). Johnston quotes the 2001 Beijing Area Study's random sampling of Beijing residents, which showed that only 8 percent of Chinese considered the revival of Japanese militarism a dominant threat to China.

27. Quoted in Ibid., 39–40.

28. Jennifer M. Lind, "Pacifism or Passing the Buck? Testing Theories of Japanese Security Policy," *International Security* 29, no. 1 (2004): 94.

29. Ibid., 96.

30. "Riben Weishenme Zongshi Buneng Shenke Fanxing?," *Renmin Wang*, 5 April 2005.

31. "Riben Zhengfu Yinggai Shenke Fanxing," *Renmin Wang*, 15 April 2005.

32. "Qin Gang: Zhongfang Buhui Chengren Suowei Donghai Dalujia "Zhongjianxian," *Renmin Wang*, 14 April 2005.

33. "Fangyin Zhuyao You San Xiang Zhongyao Chengguo," *Renmin Wang*, 12 April 2005.

34. Allen Suess Whiting, *China Eyes Japan* (Berkeley: University of California Press, 1989).

35. Jennifer Lind argues that defense spending as a percentage of GDP is a misleading statistic—rather, she relies on aggregate defense spending, corrected for PPP to argue that Japan's military expenditure is the third highest in the world. This is problematic at many levels. First, the research of the Stockholm International Peace Research Institute (SIPRI), which keeps detailed data sets of global military expenditure, shows that PPP rates are of "limited relevance" when converting military expenditure into U.S. dollars because these rates are designed to reflect the purchasing power for primarily civilian goods and services. Military expenditure, on the other hand, is used to purchase goods and services that are not typical of national consumption patterns—the price of conscripts may be lower than a typical basket of goods and services, but the prices of advanced weapons systems are much higher. So this data is unreliable if one wishes to estimate the amount of military goods and services a military budget can buy. Second, it is important to rely on more than one measure for assessments of defense spending including aggregate defense spending at market exchange rates. Stockholm International Peace Research Institute, Stockholm, Sweden, "Measuring Military Expenditure," http://www.sipri.org/research/armaments/milex/researchissues/measuring_milex.

36. SIPRI Military Expenditure Database, Information from the Stockholm International Peace Research Institute, Stockholm, Sweden, http://www.sipri.org/databases/milex.

37. SIPRI Military Expenditure Database, information from the Stockholm International Peace Research Institute, Stockholm, Sweden, http://www.sipri.org/databases/milex.

38. Thomas U. Berger, "From Sword to Chrysanthemum: Japan's Culture of Anti-Militarism," *International Security* 17, no. 4 (1993): 120.

39. Peter J. Katzenstein, *Cultural Norms and National Security: Police and Military in Post-War Japan* (Ithaca, NY: Cornell University Press, 1996), 132–38.

40. Thomas Berger, *War, Guilt, and World Politics after World War II* (Cambridge and New York: Cambridge University Press, 2012), 66.

41. He, "History, Chinese Nationalism and the Emerging Sino-Japanese Conflict."

42. Yang Daqing, "Mirror for the Future or the History Card? Understanding the 'History Problem,'" in *Chinese-Japanese Relations in the Twenty-First Century: Complementarily and Conflict*, ed. Marie Söderberg (New York: Routledge, 2003), 16.

43. Jessica Weiss, "The 2005 Anti-Japanese Protests in China and the Negotiations over UN Security Council Expansion," unpublished paper, Department of Political Science, University of California: San Diego.

44. "Riben Heshi Rang Zhongguo Zhichi Ni 'Ruchang'?," *Renmin Wang*, 9 May 2005.

45. This chapter will use Japan's involvement in China during World War II interchangeably with the second Sino-Japanese War, which lasted from 1937 to 1945, even though World War II conventionally is viewed as lasting from 1939 to 1945 based on activities in the European theater.

46. Caroline Rose, *Sino-Japanese Relations: Facing the Past, Looking to the Future?* (London, New York: RoutledgeCurzon, 2005).

47. Ibid., 4.

48. S. C. M. Paine, *The Sino-Japanese War of 1894–1895: Perceptions, Power, and Primacy* (Cambridge, New York: Cambridge University Press, 2003).

49. Whiting, *China Eyes Japan*.

50. Ibid., 33.

51. Peter Duus, Ramon Hawley Myers and Mark R. Peattie, eds., *The Japanese Informal Empire in China, 1895–1937* (Princeton: Princeton University Press, 1989).

52. Louise Young, "Imagined Empire: The Cultural Construction of Manchukuo," in *The Japanese Wartime Empire, 1931–1945*, ed. Ramon Myers, Mark Peattie, and Peter Duus (Princeton: Princeton University Press, 1996), 71.

53. Albert Feuerwerker, "Japanese Informal Imperialism in China," in *The Japanese Informal Empire in China*, ed. Duus, Myers and Peattie, 432.

54. Iris Chang, *The Rape of Nanjing: The Forgotten Holocaust of World War II* (Penguin Books, 1997).

55. Mark Eykholt, "Aggression, Victimization, and Chinese Historiography of the Nanjing Massacre," in *The Nanjing Massacre in History and Historiography*, ed. Joshua Fogel (Berkeley: University of California Press, 2000), 11.

56. Fogel, *The Nanjing Massacre in History and Historiography*.

57. G. Rozman, "China's Changing Images of Japan, 1989–2001: The Struggle to Balance Partnership and Rivalry," *International Relations of the Asia-Pacific* 2 (2002).

58. Yang, "Mirror for the Future or the History Card?," 10.

59. He, "History, Chinese Nationalism and the Emerging Sino-Japanese Conflict." 2.

60. Whiting, *China Eyes Japan*.

61. See Yang, "Mirror for the Future or the History Card?," 12; He, "History, Chinese Nationalism and the Emerging Sino-Japanese Conflict."

62. He, "History, Chinese Nationalism and the Emerging Sino-Japanese Conflict," 8.

63. Ibid.

64. Ibid., 6.

65. Peter Hays Gries, "China's 'New Thinking' on Japan," *China Quarterly* 184 (2005).

66. Nicholas Kristof, "The Problem of Memory," *Foreign Affairs* 77, no. 6 (1998).

67. Japan has periodically conveyed remorse and self-reflection. Prime Minister Tomiichi Murayama used the word "apology" for the first time in 1995, while Prime Minister Junichiro Koizumi apologized for Japanese imperialism in 2005, but these attempts are undercut by hard-line Japanese politicians and intellectuals. It was particularly galling to the Chinese, for example, when the Japanese Diet refused to pass a proposal to apologize for Japan's war crimes.

68. T. Beal, Y. Nozaki and J. Yang, "Ghost of the Past: The Japanese History Textbook Controversy," *New Zealand Journal of Asian Studies* 3, no. 2 (2001).

69. Rose, *Sino-Japanese Relations*, 55–61.

70. John Ikenberry, "Japan's History Problem," *Washington Post*, 17 August 2006.

71. Gries, "China's 'New Thinking' on Japan," 847.

72. Jessica Weiss, "Powerful Patriots: Nationalism, Diplomacy, and the Strategic Logic of Anti-Foreign Protest" (Ph.D. dissertation, University of California, San Diego, 2008).

73. The *China People's Daily* is available online in both Chinese and English. For this analysis, only the Chinese language website at http://www.people.com.cn/ was searched.

74. The search threw up not only articles and editorials but also interviews and web postings. All of these were coded and sorted for the analysis.

75. "Pinglunyuan Zaixian: Chengwei Changren Lishiguo, Riben Xuyao Daode Yingxiangli," *Renmin Wang*, 17 September 2004.

76. "Junshi Guancha: Riben De Junshi Fazhan He Changren Lishiguo Zhi Meng," *Renmin Wang*, 15 December 2004.

77. "Xin Jingbao: Chengdan Guoji Zeren Xianyao Zhengshi Lishi," *Renmin Wang*, 27 March 2005.

78. "Riben Dui Quanqiu Qianming Wudongyuzhong Jingxinsheji Sanbu Zou Zhanlue," *Renmin Wang*, 1 April 2005.

79. "Riben Bugai Chengwei Anlihui Changren Lishiguo," *Renmin Wang*, 1 April 2005.

80. "Waijiaobu Fayanren Qin Gang Jiu Ri Jiaokeshu Wenti Deng Da Jizhe Wen," *Renmin Wang*, 5 April 2005.

81. "Qianwan Qianming Juji Riben," *Renmin Wang*, 7 April 2005.

82. "Daizhe 20 Wan 'Zhongguo Weianfu' De Xuelei, Riben You He Yanmian Zuo Anlihui Changren?," *Renmin Wang*, 11 April 2005.

83. "Zhongguo Biaoming Lishi Wenti Juebu Rangbu Guoji Meiti Pingshu Zhongri Guanxi, Renwei Zhongguo Zai Lishi Wenti Shang Juebu Rangbu," *Renmin Wang*, 14 April 2005.

84. "Zhongri Guanxi Zhibing Xu Zhaodao Binggen," *Renmin Wang*, 24 April 2005.

85. "Riben Heshi Rang Zhongguo Zhichi Ni Ruchang?," *Renmin Wang*, 9 May 2005.

86. "3 Ri Guandian Jicui: Guoxueyan: Dashan Sheng Ge Xiaohaozi?," *Renmin Wang*, 3 June 2005.

87. "Meiguofang Buzhang Youguan Zhongguo Junfei Shuofa Haowu Genju," *Renmin Wang*, 7 June 2005.

88. "Riben Yi Qiangshi Zitai Shitan Zhongguo Yu Shijie Rongrendu," *Renmin Wang*, 3 August 2005.

89. "Jinian Kangzhan Shengli 60 Zhounian Meiti Pinglunji," *Renmin Wang*, 16 August 2005.

90. "Riben Yi Nanyi Weixie Zhongguo," *Renmin Wang*, 4 August 2005.

91. Available online at http://military.people.com.cn/GB/8221/51757/52478/index.html.

92. The chapters were successively published on *Renmin Wang* in August 2005.

93. "Zhongguo Daodi Chu Shenme Pai?," *Renmin Wang*, 29 August 2005.

94. "Bu Shenke Fanxing Lishi, Ri Ruhe Jin Anlihui," *Zhongguo Xinwen Wang*, http://www.sina.com.cn, 22 September 2004.

95. "Hanguo: Riben Ho Changrenxi Bixu Xian Gaibian Dui Yazhou Taidu," *Zhongguo Guangbowang*, http://www.sina.com.cn, 27 October 2004.

96. "Ying Xian Qingsuan Zuie De Quinlueshi Chaoxian Zhiyi Riben Mou "Chang," *Han Wang*, http://sina.com.cn, 4 October 2004.

97. "Yu Huo Anlihui Changren Lishiguo Xiwei Linguo Wu Hecai Riben Gangga," *Xinhua Wang*, http://www.sina.com.cn, 28 March 2005.

98. Weiss, "The 2005 Anti-Japanese Protests in China," 28–31.

99. Ibid., 33.

Conclusion

1. "BJP Raises Din over Manmohan's Colonial Musings," *Economic Times*, 14 July 2005.

2. Zheng Wang, *Never Forget National Humiliation: Historical Memory in Chinese Politics and Foreign Relations* (New York: Columbia University Press, 2012), 144.

3. Quoted in ibid., 144–45.

4. Interview with Ashok Malik, political columnist, 22 June 2012, New Delhi, India.

5. "China, Olympic Victim?," *The Economist*, 18 August 2012.

6. Zheng Wang, *Never Forget National Humiliation*, 154.

7. Quoted in "China's Olympic Soul Searching: What the Games Have Taught the Country," *Daily Beast*, http://www.thedailybeast.com/articles/2012/08/12/china-s-olympic-soul-searching-what-the-games-have-taught-the-country.html.

8. "Cong Lundun Aoyunhui Kan Xifang Yi Xie Ren Dui Zhongguo De Aoman Pianjian," *Renmin Wang*, 13 August 2012.

9. "Historical Weakness Creates China's Gold Medal Fixation," *Global Times*, 8 August 2012.

10. Zheng Wang, *Never Forget National Humiliation*, 151–52.

11. "China Faces Charges of Colonialism In Africa," *New York Times*, 28 January 2007.

12. "China's Hu Rejects 'Colonial' Tag on South Africa Visit," *Channel News Asia*, 7 February 2007.

13. Nicholas Kristof, "Zimbabwe and the Causes of African Poverty," *New York Times*, 10 April 2010.

14. Nicholas Dirks, "Foreword," in Bernard S. Cohn, *Colonialism and Its Forms of Knowledge: The British in India* (Princeton: Princeton University Press, 1996), ix.

15. Martha Finnemore and Kathryn Sikkink, "International Norm Dynamics and Political Change," *International Organization* 52, no. 4 (1998): 887–917.

16. Christopher J. Hemmer and Peter Katzenstein, "Why Is There No NATO in Asia? Collective, Identity, Regionalism and, the Origins of Multilateralism," *International Organization* 56, no. 3 (2002): 592.

17. Judith M. Brown, *Nehru: A Political Life* (New Haven and London: Yale University Press, 2003), 263.

18. Mohammed Ayoob, "The Third World in the System of States: Acute Schizophrenia or Growing Pains?," *International Studies Quarterly* 33, no. 3 (March 1989): 67–79.

19. Edward E. Azar and Chung-in Moon, eds., *National Security in the Third World: The Management of Internal and External Threats* (University of Maryland: Center for International Development and Conflict, 1988), 3–6.

20. Louise Fawcett and Yezid Sayigh, eds., *The Third World beyond the Cold War: Continuity and Change* (Oxford: Oxford University Press, 1999), 6; Barry Buzan, "People, States and Fear: The National Security Problem in the Third World," in *National Security in the Third World*, ed. Azar and Moon.

21. Donald J. Puchala, "Third World Thinking and Contemporary International Relations," in *International Relations Theory and the Third World,* ed. Edward E. Azar and Chung-in Moon (New York: St. Martin's Press, 1998), 138–44.

22. Amitav Acharya, *Whose Ideas Matter: Agency and Power in Asian Regionalism* (Ithaca, NY, and London: Cornell University Press, 2009), 3.

23. Ibid., 28, 44.

24. Christopher Clapham, "Sovereignty and the Third World State," in Robert Jackson, ed., *Sovereignty at the Millennium* (Oxford: Blackwell Publishers, 1999).

25. Tom Christensen, "Pride, Pressure and Politics: The Roots of China's Worldview," in *In the Eyes of the Dragon: China Views the World*, ed. Yong Deng and Fei-Ling Wang (Lanham, MD: Rowman and Littlefield, 1999), 243.

Index

Studies in Asian Security

Amitav Acharya, Chief Editor, American University
David Leheny, Chief Editor, Princeton University